THE MAN WHO
STRAIGHTENED
NAILS

THE MAN WHO
STRAIGHTENED
NAILS

A daughter remembers . . .

MARY ABBOTT

iUniverse, Inc.
Bloomington

The Man Who Straightened Nails
A Daughter Remembers . . .

Few names have been changed. These are my memories.

iUniverse books may be ordered through booksellers or by contacting:

iUniverse
1663 Liberty Drive
Bloomington, IN 47403
www.iuniverse.com
1-800-Authors (1-800-288-4677)

ISBN: 978-1-4697-5834-3 (sc)
ISBN: 978-1-4697-5835-0 (ebk)

Printed in the United States of America

iUniverse rev. date: 02/28/2012

CONTENTS

In Memory of My Parents

Few names have been changed. These are my memories.

INTRODUCTION

Everyone in the small community of Vandorf knew the Burnett family. Stewart was regarded as an honest man whose hard work was legendary. His wife Helen took her duties as a homemaker and mother seriously, as if they were a long dreamed about career choice. The three children were a little wild, but it didn't seem to bother the parents too much. Many people envied the family and their seemingly perfect life, others thought them slightly eccentric. This was my family.

My parents were the ones always ready to lend a hand to those less fortunate. Without even being aware of it they followed the so called 'Golden Rule'. They gave their children freedom, imagination, love, protection and a donkey in the kitchen. All of the necessities of life were ours without a care in the world.

To me heaven could be no better.

When we became adults we brought with us weddings, babies, family celebrations and laughter, always the laughter. Some say we were lucky, but our luck came in human form. We had my Dad. We had Stewart.

Then one day in August the laughter stopped and the lights went out. When they came on again I found myself in a creepy, alien land, with nowhere to hide, floundering, looking for answers.

Not for one second did I think it would take so long for the answers to reveal themselves.

CHAPTER I

SOWING THE SEEDS

OF A FAMILY

On the evening of October 15, 1954, the radio stations were following the path and destruction of a hurricane that was heading north towards Toronto. Originating in the Atlantic Ocean it had already killed over one thousand people in Haiti and another ninety-five in the United States. Before it was over eighty-one more people would lose their lives in the Toronto area. It was given the name Hazel.

My parents felt compelled to venture out before it got too bad. The wind and rain were just beginning and Dad had to check for damage, both on his farm and those of our neighbours in the small, tightly-knit community. He scanned the sky and studied the direction the wind was blowing. Would it hit here or would it just fizzle out like storms so often do?

My older brother Bob, all of fifteen, was left to babysit his two younger siblings, myself seven and our brother Ron six. Late in the evening Bob came into our rooms and roused us from gentle sleep. "There's going to be a terrible storm, probably the worst we've ever had. It's going to hit soon so get up and leave your pajamas on, there's no time to get dressed." He had decided to take us to the hired hand's house till Mom and Dad got home. He told us that because the house was located behind the barn it would be better protected from the wind. Would the barn sheltering a tiny house be better protection than our huge, brick fortress of a home? Maybe, but I believe that Bob did what he thought best to keep us safe and that he didn't want to be alone in the big house with the wind and the sky, making noises he'd never heard before. He headed out to the cottage-like home, head lowered against the wind and rain, carrying a little kid under each arm. When we arrived at the little haven he put us in bed with the children of the hired hand.

Mom and Dad arrived home around midnight, just at the peak of the storm. It was so badly flooded by this time that it was impossible to get their new Dodge, a vehicle as big as a bus, up the lane. We were awakened for the second time that night. The wind was all around us, making my Dad stagger as he took me in his arms and wrapped me in his coat. At one point I told him that my toes were cold and he said, "We'll fix that," and stuffed my toes in his pocket. We must have looked like a pretty pathetic group as we made our way down the muddy, flooded lane to our house. I was wrapped in my Dad's strong arms, Mom had Ron, and Bob was probably getting hell for moving us in the first place. I like to think he was getting praise. Toes in the pocket, Dad and I always laughed about that, remembered it. It somehow seemed very important to both of us.

Hurricane Hazel caused massive flooding. The Holland Marsh, the major supplier of vegetables for Canadian consumers, was completely under water. We suffered less damage than most of our neighbors, so Dad spent the next few weeks at friends' farms helping out where ever he was needed. It was a gathering of the community; husbands and wives deciding which family had suffered the most damage and starting to rebuild there. The women provided the food and often took frightened children home with them. The men did the hard, physical labor, putting houses and barns back together and what must have been the worst, the very, very tedious job of picking up debris. Not much could be done about the flooding, just wait for the water to subside on its own, and pray that we didn't have an early winter with ice.Over fifty years later my Mom mentioned that she couldn't believe that she and Dad had left us kids alone in the middle of a hurricane. That was the first time she ever brought it up, made it sound like a bad thing, something she should feel guilt about. It was no big deal to us. The farm always came first.

If there was anything remotely fortunate about Hazel it was that it hit in October. The crops were in and the cattle and other animals safe in the barn, However, Dad didn't need the unexpected work load. Running a successful farm is a constant struggle. No let-up, ever. During the winter months the animals had to be fed and their manure cleaned twice a day. Dad had to be home by four-thirty on the dot, according to 'Stewart Schedule', to do the chores, every day, seven days a week. If we were half an hour late returning in the evening, we would exit the car to the sound of cows and pigs calling for their supper, which was almost like a melody after listening to Dad's complaints all the way home about being late and whose fault it was (usually Moms.)

Spring, that's when the back breaking work really began and the dawn to dusk days. It really makes so much sense when you think about it, how it all falls into a precise order like nature itself. Rough, weed covered, hard dirt is coaxed into a soil as fine and soft as sand, eventually ready to nourish a tiny seed. Depending on the weather and the care with which the soil was prepared, you would get a good crop or a bad crop. If you got a bad crop there wouldn't be enough feed for the animals over the winter months.

Spring was also the time when the birthing process began. The cattle were out in the fields now so had to be constantly watched for the arrival of a calf. It really was amazing the number of cattle that had trouble bringing a new life into the world. Often a calf just wouldn't come and if Dad couldn't get it out himself he would have to resort to using a tractor and rope. A dead calf would be a loss, but the death of a cow would be a calamity. And there were the baby pigs, so cute you could almost kiss their little button noses, but every time you picked one up, no matter how young it was, it would let out horrid, high pitched squeals and wiggle around so much there was no pleasure at all in holding it. The day would come when one by one, Dad would have to manually remove their teeth and shove in a teaspoonful of supplement, all the while a miserable, unpredictable sow would be trying to jump out of her enclosure to get to her piglets. The noise was indescribable. The sows seemed to give birth easily, but then they would often lie down on top of their young, giving them a quick and hopefully painless death.

In the summer Dad's fields would be squares of green, like the terraces of countries we'd see in magazines. Nothing was ever out of place, not even a piece of paper blowing in the wind. Old Mrs. Offenhem, who lived close by, once told me that she had just returned from a trip to Ireland and how beautiful the scenery was, so orderly and precise. She had turned to her friend and said "Stewart Burnett must be Irish." I guess that's why he won the silver tray for the Best Kept Farm in York County.

My Dad loved every moment of it. He needed perfection, and knew instinctively how to achieve it. Aside from his three meals a day, which had to be at the exact time, eight, twelve and six, he was working. I have a picture that Mom took of him fast asleep in his chair, head in hand, legs drawn up underneath him. It was so unusual to see him sleep during the day that she felt the need to take a picture. It had to be a Sunday, his only day of semi-rest.

If on a rare occasion my Father could find nothing to do, he would straighten nails. On one side of him would be a tin of old, rusty, bent nails, on the other side would be another tin where he would put the nails after he had cleaned them and hammered them out to make them useable again, like new. He would salvage every nail he came across, pulling them out of beams, barn boards, trees and long forgotten fence lines. He even found old forged square cut nails, antiques to others, but to him they were worth saving because you never knew when you might need a square cut nail. When he was still doing this in his eighties we kids just couldn't understand it. He'd done it his whole life. How much did nails cost? It didn't matter. Dad didn't like to spend money and took it to the extreme. If you didn't need it you didn't buy it, and he needed very, very little. Money was something to be accumulated, to pass onto the next generation to give them a leg up in life, like his father and his grandfather had done. It was the Scottish way.

Just to be sure that Dad didn't go completely overboard in his money saving, God, in a rather cruel trick, gave him Mom. My

Mothers main interest was shopping and I don't think I ever knew a woman that could spend money like she did. As Bob once said in a speech at their 60th anniversary, "They are a couple well matched. He can't stop making money and she can't stop spending it." She was a loving wife and mother, passionately protective towards her children. She had the mistaken belief that we could do no wrong. My Mother worked hard but never complained, and had that rare ability to laugh at life, just throw back her head and laugh. She was beautiful with a dark complexion and coal black hair. Her perfect white teeth lasted a lifetime. She had style. When I was born, blue eyed and very fair, the doctor told her that if he didn't know my father he wouldn't believe that I was her baby. A ridiculous statement, but you get the idea. She was so very dark and I had such light skin and was blonde, like my Dad.

Just before her accidental death in 2002 she was all excited because she had made an appointment to have Botox injected into her face to get rid of what few wrinkles she had. Mom didn't hesitate to head to the plastic surgeon when the need arose so when she heard about this new injectable that was safe and almost immediately erased wrinkles she was ready to go. Botox was relatively new back then, it hadn't hit mainstream society to the extent it has today and I knew very little about it. I explained that it was poison, and that it could be very dangerous. I regret that I talked her out of it. She would have been thrilled with the results. She was 82, and I had to go and burst her balloon.

Of course it wasn't always like this. Times were very hard during my parents early years of marriage. There was no money and Dad did the chores by the light of lanterns. Bob was born during their first year. He was born on Granny Burnett's dining room table. I used to imagine this scene over and over again. It was like a movie I played in my head. I pictured Granny bustling about in her quiet way, water boiling on the wood stove, and Mom, so naive about such matters, probably thinking she was about to die. The men would be in the other room waiting for news or the lusty cry of a newborn. The images would whirl around in my young head, reminding me of our pioneer roots and that I was born right where I was meant to be. Mom never talked about what it was like when she had Bob, but I wish that I had asked her to tell me about it. Now I'll never know. There's no one left to tell the story.

Bob was the oldest of us three kids. He had it the toughest. He was the first born, subject to the work ethic demanded from the eldest son of a farmer. He was Dad's main help, and unfortunately the common belief during the difficult war years was, 'spare the rod, and spoil the child'. He, at such a young age, was the one who had to help with chores, chop wood for heat and cooking and help Dad race the elements to plant and get the crops in, all without the use of modern machinery. It seems almost impossible that the only 'machine' was a team of well-trained work horses that had to move together in unison. Dad would work the fields, the horses hitched up with the reins lying unattended on the seat of a plough or wagon. They knew the commands 'Gee' and 'Haw' (right and left) as well as a dog knew the command to sit or stay. Dad would yell when a change of direction was required and they would start to turn, the two of them in partnership, like a well-choreographed dance. The invention of various machines made a farmer's life a little easier, however, it was so sad to see the remarkable work horse replaced by an unpredictable tractor that spewed exhaust fumes into your face.

I was born eight years after Bob and my father and I had a very close bond, right from the beginning. Relatives and neighbors would whisper, "Stewarts making a fool of himself over that child." We couldn't get enough of each other. I was in his arms whenever possible. As soon as I could walk I would leave my bed and still half asleep make my way to the breakfast table and his lap. "Good morning girlie," he'd say as he cleared off a corner of his plate for Mom to put my breakfast on. This continued until my Mother decided that I was too old for such babyish behavior and made me sit in a chair, like my brothers.

Ron was born less than a year after me. He had a bit of a temper from a very young age and would fight at the drop of a hat. Certain phrases from Dad would change him from a mere lad of three to a cursing sailor. Mom used to say that she was truly afraid that Ron would develop psychological problems due to Dad's teasing. At dinner Ron would say, "Pass the damn ketchup or I'll upset the damn table." Things would start to slide as his end of the table began to rise and he quickly got the ketchup. Dad would laugh, and Mom would sternly tell him, "Stewart, that's no way to raise a child." There were seldom any consequences, especially if it happened at home, away from the prying eyes of the neighbors. Mom would try to play the strict parent, a role that she didn't have the temperament for, and she would end up laughing about episodes that really should have resulted in some kind of punishment. Dad could never, ever, resist the lure of her laughter.

An early memory, one I hold close, is my Mother's voice, shocked, that Dad would put me, at four years old, on one of our huge work horses. They were massive, white animals named Jim and Doll. He'd hoist me up, and the horses would wander down to the meadow to graze then return at noon for a drink. That's when he'd get me off. In his mind there was nothing that could happen. Every day that it occurred, Mom saw a situation that could have dire results. A fall would be disastrous, if not fatal. They'd spar back and forth, but when it came to the farm and his trust in most animals Dad usually won.

Alone astride that magnificent animal, I daydreamed, watched butterflies, birds, groundhogs, the clouds and as the horse strolled from one clump of grass to another I would sit up straight, take hold of the mane and would be riding, at least for a step or two. Often I would feel sleepy, thread my small fingers through Doll's mane and just lay my head down. She was so broad I felt perfectly safe.

It was where I was meant to be and I knew it even then. I spent my entire childhood and well into adulthood astride a pony or horse. I was passionate about riding. It was the only place I felt truly comfortable in my skin. Dad understood this. He would just shrug off Mom's hysterics about the morning rides. Nothing would happen. He trusted his gentle giant to take care of his most valuable cargo. I think it was about this time that my Mom began to give up, to just let fate, or God, look after us.

Eventually my Father was financially stable enough to buy a farm on Wellington Street close to Aurora. This was the place that would shape all of my memories; over two hundred acres of playground, a fantasy world. We two younger kids didn't have a care in our little heads, just ideas, the kind of ideas and plans that every child should have. Bob was that much older and he had no desire to join us in our adventures, didn't even particularly care for the farm in general. He always had more important things to do. By sixteen it seemed his only interest was cars. He spent all of his spare time in the garage. Bob could get very angry when things didn't run smoothly and there was often the sound of a thrown wench hitting the garage wall. He, like Ron, had a bit of a temper. I had no temper, but was often moody and sullen.

One weekend we had company and I had to sleep with Bob. I figured that everything would be fine as long as I didn't make him mad. I didn't want to disturb my brother by getting up to go to the bathroom and while I was thinking about it, I wet the bed. What to do? I figured out a fool-proof plan. If I slept all night with my leg holding back the urine like a dam, he'd never know. It seemed to be under control, the urine was staying on my side of the bed. I fell into a restless dream filled sleep and when I woke in the morning it was to loud complaints to Mom about having to sleep with a kid that was far too old to be wetting the bed. Another time Bob caught a mouse and put it in a guitar as a cage. When he left for school Ron and I were given warnings not to go near that mouse. We did, it bit my finger and escaped. When Bob got home from school and went to look at his mouse Ron and I were nowhere to be found. We really did test his patience and wreck his stuff. No doubt about it, we were Bob's cross to bear.

So there we were, a family, back in the days when if a fire truck or ambulance went by you got in your car to follow to see which of your neighbors was in trouble. Our days were full. In the quiet afternoons when Bob was at school and Dad in the fields, Ron and I would lay in bed with Mom. We played 'I Spy with My Little Eye' and sang, 'How Much is that Doggie in the Window'? Ron got to do the required 'ruff ruffs'. Over fifty years later, I can still see and hear the three of us. I can feel Mom's laughter, her joy in us.

Dad was always driving the tractor pulling some contraption to work the land. The contentment on his face made him look like a king on his throne. All day he'd drive, often into the evening, leaving a field as smooth and clean as a millionaire's lawn. When I got old enough to actually think, I would watch him, and wonder what *he* was thinking as he drove for all those hours. I could not imagine his mind being still when he was so consumed with work. I began to believe that he wasn't thinking at all, just watching nature unfold before his eyes. Then one day it hit me. In all likelihood he was just looking for more work, a fence that needed mending, a tree branch that had fallen in the night and had to be removed, or a ground hog's hole that needed taking care of. He was complex in his simplicity.

There is nothing in this world like the smell of newly cut hay, although freshly mown grass is a close second. Summer was a time for swimming in the pond, looking for pollywogs, and sometimes, as a special treat, a cold, sugar filled bottle of highly colored Orange Crush. Every child drank that stuff. It was deemed to be 'healthier' than the other pops.

There would still be some hay in the barn left over from winter and Ron and I spent a lot of time making forts. When we built forts the chance of being crushed just added to the adventure. Our hay-bale forts were works of art, although shimmying through a very narrow entrance into a cleared out square scared me. It was very claustrophobic getting into the forts. Well into adulthood, I would dream of the terror of squeezing through those small openings. There was another terror associated with our fort building, snakes.

My Mom had instilled in us kids, at least the two younger ones, such a fear of snakes that it became irrational. It was so unlike Ron and me because we were not frightened of any other living creature. Bob must have missed out on the childhood trauma because he didn't seem to mind them. Even before Dad put me on Doll, before anything reared in my innocent child's brain, I remember my Mother out in the vegetable garden, screaming in absolute terror at the sight of a little garter snake. Did Mothers scream? Weren't they supposed to be the ones that soothed our screams? It would have to be something truly horrendous to cause such a reaction.

Once, before we were in school, Ron and I took a hatchet from the shed and went wild animal hunting. We were strolling back towards the pond when we came upon a curled garter snake. We were so startled that we threw the hatchet on the snake and ran as fast as we possibly could. We got no sympathy from Dad when we got home. He was so mad that we'd taken the hatchet that he told us to get our arses back to where we'd left it and bring it back. We were petrified, crying in fear as we walked down the hill. We strolled slowly, the terror almost immobilizing. We got lucky, the snake was gone. We grabbed the hatchet and ran home to breathlessly tell our Mother the whole story and what Dad had made us do. She comforted us with hugs and murmurs of love. There were no hugs from Dad. Even today, decades later, if my life isn't going well or something is bothering me I will have nightmares about snakes. After a night of terror, thinking snakes are in my bed wrapping themselves around my body, I will wonder what's going on, what small or imagined crisis is causing me to feel such sub-conscious fear.

Haying season was when my Mother would send me out to the field with a pitcher of cold lemonade that my Father would devour like a man dying of thirst. Actually, haying time would be pure hell to all of us but Dad. It was the dirtiest, heaviest, most rotten job in the world and to make it worse it was done during the hottest weeks of the summer. As kids it meant a ride back to the hay field on an empty wagon with our constant companion, Laddie, a dog whose mission in life was to protect us. He joined in all of our adventures. He ran along beside us, and often seemed to be laughing with unbridled joy. Like us. When we found something interesting his nose was right in the middle of it and when we cried he lay down between, us, eyes darting from one to the other, waiting for the drama to end.

Ron and I would hunt for animals, swim in the dirty pond, and catch minnows in a jar, while Dad and Bob loaded the wagon. When the wagon was full we'd climb to the top. Often it would lean on the side of a hill and threaten to tip over. We had square bales back then and they were so heavy that it was an effort for a grown man to pick one up (except for Dad who would take one in each hand when he was loading the wagon alone.) Bob would tease us. "If this wagon tips over you two will be crushed under all the bales because you're so small. I'm bigger so I can jump out of the way. And if we hit hydro wires don't look at me to put the fire out." Banter, back and forth, that was part of the excitement.

If Dad could get no one to help him load the wagon it wasn't such a great day for Ron and me. Starting when we were very young he would drag us from our summer adventures and make us steer the tractor while he loaded the wagon himself. We were so little we couldn't turn the heavy wheel, but the hay had to be in the barn before rain; there was always a deadline. Our job was to keep the tractor straight, then when we had to turn a corner or stop Dad would jump on. The only real problem was ground hog holes. If we would see one looming we were helpless. We would yell for Dad to come and drive around it. There was no way we could turn a tractor, pulling a wagon loaded with hay, safely around a huge hole in the ground. We just didn't have the strength. A few times when we either didn't want to call on Dad again or were feeling especially cocky, we'd try to do it ourselves, try to turn the wheel together. The results were upset loads, and occasionally the very worst that could happen, a broken axle. Frustration would cause Dad to blow up, tell us to get the hell out of the way, and we'd be off again, not an ounce of sympathy for Dad who would be unloading a tipped wagon so he could fix the axle, then reloading it again, by himself.

Cows, horses, goats, pigs, even a circus pony. We benefited from the fact that our Father would buy virtually any moving creature if he could make a buck on it. One day I was in my room when I heard a commotion downstairs in the kitchen. Mom was sounding very agitated. "Stewart, you get that filthy beast out of this house right this minute." I ran downstairs, my excitement bubbling over at the thought of a filthy beast in the kitchen. There stood my Father, eyes sparkling and casually leaning against the freezer. He was holding one end of a rope; the other end was loosely draped around the neck of a donkey. We laughed together as he hoisted me onto it's back. My mother was by this time swishing at the animal with a tea towel. Dad told her with a slight grin on his face, "You'd better look out. A donkey can give a mean kick, use both hind legs." Over the next few days my enthusiasm slowly began to dwindle. The donkey could barely be described as a moving creature because when I'd climb on, it wouldn't move, not one step. I had to plead with Ron, bribe him, to walk behind poking it in the 'ass' with the pitch fork. Its huge ears would flatten against its neck in anger and it would give me the gift of a forward motion of a couple of steps. I didn't cry when the donkey went, Dad had probably only paid a buck for it and sold it for two.

There would never be any sympathy when we'd go out to the barn after school to find one of our pets gone. Mom, always the jokester, took to calling these occasions 'the day Ron's calf became dad's cow', probably because Ron would scream and cry and swear and give my parents their entertainment for the day. The calves we loved most, the ones that we took to heart, were the Jerseys. They were so delicate and beautiful, just like baby deer. We coddled them and let them suck our fingers, marvelling at their gentleness. Then one morning we'd go skipping out to the barn to find our pet gone, and Mom's little jingle ringing in our ears.

All three of us kids often brought home stray dogs and Dad had the most ingenious way of getting rid of them. He'd wait until around three when school was letting out, put the dog on a rope and ask the kids walking home if they wanted a dog. It never failed. We had two good dogs that were keepers. Bob's 'Rusty' and Ron and my 'Laddie'.

We were pretty much allowed to come and go as we pleased on the farm, the only refrain we would hear day after day was to shut the gates, the barn door, and don't go in the pigpen. All animals were ours to do with what we pleased, except the pigs. Dad warned us over and over again not to go into the pigpen, but of course we did because when you lifted the heavy food bin door there was often a mouse, and if you acted quickly enough you could catch it. I finally understood the danger of the pigs when years later I went to get Jenny, my beautiful Welsh pony, from the pasture only to find her entrails hanging to the ground from a huge bloody hole in her belly. While she had been innocently grazing, oblivious, she'd wandered too close to a boar. Dad had to pull out his wallet for that one.

One animal we all had a great deal of respect for was Curly the bull. He was not a nice bull and would charge anyone who entered his domain. Dad seemed to like Curly. He'd say to kids, who appeared to be fast runners, "Go and see if that's a ground hog hole over there by the tree." then he'd laugh merrily as the poor innocent would run for the nearest fence. The one kid that just didn't seem to learn was Andy, dad's unpaid young helper. Andy lived just up the road. He had a very difficult home life, so he started appearing at the farm after school and all summer. He and Dad enjoyed each other's company even though Andy was younger than Ron. They seemed to form a bond. Andy was as bad tempered as Curly, and could curse like no child ever should. Dad would tease him until he would throw a fi and face red with anger storm off home, swearing he'd never be back. Dad would laugh till tears filled his eyes. The more out of control Andy became the more pleasure my Father got. The next day Andy would always show up. His anger usually involved Curly, snakes or a dead animal. Mom would warn Dad that one day Andy wouldn't come back, but he always did.

Before the warm days of spring and the freedom of summer, there was that one very special day when Ron and I would make our way back to the pond to see how it had fared over the winter. Was the water level high or low? What new growth would be around it? Would the little island in the centre be there this year? Any sign of pollywogs, new birds busy making nests? Was it going to be a good swimming year?

That pond centered greatly for every member of the family. We swam in it, and in the winter played hockey and figure skated on the bumpy ice. One time Mom actually drove a ski-do though the ice. She was laughing so hard we thought she was crying and hurt. One afternoon after school Ron and I skated far into the night and it got colder and darker. Trying to take my skates off and put my boots on I started to cry, tears freezing on my cheeks. My fingers wouldn't work so, skates still on my feet I headed across the field toward the road feeling more defeated with every step. Ron was far ahead of me and I was stumbling behind, falling often. Finally reaching the road I saw a familiar car, slowly driving up and down the road looking for us in the dark. It was Mom. When we got home there was hot chocolate on the stove. This episode wasn't terribly important, except that I could have frozen to death, but it stayed with me, a reminder that my Mom would always be there to save me.

For whatever reason, I fail to remember, Ron and I once caught enough frogs back at the pond to fill a huge, plastic, dry cleaning bag full to the brim. It took two of us to carry it the half mile or so back to the house. Can you imagine the ones on the bottom? Just as we got to the front veranda the bag broke. By the next day there wasn't a frog to be seen. Where had they all gone? Now, I wonder, "Why?" What great plan was in our little minds to spend a day catching all those frogs? We'd planned it all out because we'd taken the bag with us. Did we think we could sell them? Were we planning on digging a pond closer to the house? Digging a new pond was something we talked about a lot.

Riding along the paths made by the cattle when they went to the pond for a drink was the best. The air was filled with imagination. Even as a child there was that need to embrace it all, hold on to it. I often would lie back on Jenny, staring up at blue sky and sun. Like those times so many years ago when I would be lulled to sleep in Doll's huge cradle. In my heart I owned these special times. They were mine and would last forever. Nothing could ever take them away. At such a young age I truly believed that. I had no reason not to.

As an adult, during a melancholy time, I'd walk back to the pond, avoiding the hundreds of cow plops along the path. After my

Mother died and I was staying with Dad I'd feel the need to get out of the house and away from the sorrow and I'd always find myself at the pond where I would sit, feel the pain drift away and be replaced by joyful memories.

My Mom didn't always get to avoid the running of the farm. Often after supper we'd head out as a family to pull mustard plants from the oat field. Ron and I did very little picking, there was just too much to see and do. A rabbit hole would keep us engrossed for over an hour as we tried to figure out how to scare the rabbit out so we could catch it. Bob didn't enjoy the mustard picking as much as Ron and I because there was nothing for him to do but pick mustard, then his sinus's and face would swell up, the result of allergies. Bob soon stopped the mustard outings completely. He was driving now and started to go out more often, 'carousing' as Mom called it, 'with a bad crowd'.

Mom was so paranoid about what her eldest son was up to that one evening my parents put us two younger ones in the backseat of the car and actually followed Bob to a joint in Newmarket called 'Bucket of Blood.' Mom sat in the darkened car and fretted. "Stewart, look at that girl in the tight pants, I don't know how she can move, she can't be more than sixteen and look at that one with her hair all piled up, teetering on high heels . . . and they're all smoking."

Bob actually got arrested for shooting off flame throwers from his car's exhaust on the main street of Newmarket. I think there were a couple more arrests. Ron and I were thrilled, Mom and Dad not so much. When he got a Harley there were all these tough looking bikers around, but they only looked tough, they were gentle and kind and very, very funny, especially Tom, Bob's best friend. One Halloween day he came to the door and Mom said, "Tom it's not night time yet, you shouldn't have your mask on so early." Tom just grinned. Bob enjoyed those years with the bikers, and always owned a Harley. He was as reckless in his way as Ron and I were in ours.

Lord knows what those two teenagers would be up to that Halloween night, probably something far more sinister than when Dad and friends, all of them in the early years of marriage and therefore somewhat mature, were pushing over a farmer's outhouse and the farmer appeared on the front porch with his shot gun. They all ran, but Dad got literally 'clothes lined' by the clothes line and was caught.

Because Bob was much older, I can't recall us doing very much together as a family, the five of us. I only remember him as a teenager, someone I watched from a distance. He had a completely separate life from us two younger kids. When I finally had to grow up, he became a friend and ally that I often turned to when I needed help in the unfamiliar world of adulthood.

Our Dad was constantly on the go, farming in the day and going to meetings at night. He hardly seemed to have time to breathe, yet he didn't act busy, if that makes any sense. We never heard him complain about too much to do, he loved it, and it's what kept him happy. He did most of the repairs at the church and successfully ran for Council. He was elected Reeve. He became a Mason, and remained a Mason for over fifty years. In his later years he liked to say that he had served on one committee or another for over sixty years-without a break.

On top of everything else Mom and Dad had a vibrant social life and many nights Ron and I were left in the capable hands of our big brother who would immediately disappear with a stern warning not to tell our parents. Ron and I would go directly to the basement and dig out our signs, hidden just for these occasions. We would go to the end of the lane and wave them at every car that went by. They read 'WILD ANIMALS FOR SALE, ORDERS TAKEN'. And once when that enterprise wasn't doing well we dragged all of our clothes out in an attempt to sell them. When our parents would come home Ron and I would be sound asleep and Bob would be innocently watching television.

We laughed often, as adults, about Mom and Dad's parenting skills. They never worried too much. If they hadn't seen their youngest two for several hours they thought it quite normal to just call the dog. The direction the dog came from was an indication as to where we would be. They truly believed that this was a good babysitting strategy.

Ron and I fought, viciously and physically. I'm sure on some days Mom would think out loud, "The curses coming from that garage are disgraceful and those other two are rolling around on the front lawn kicking and biting and scratching. I hope none of the neighbours drop in." Then she'd go back to her work, usually baking pies. Mom and Dad didn't bother trying to break us up when we had these little exchanges. Their attitude was fight yourselves out.

The worst parenting idea, by far, was to buy Ron a B.B. gun. Why would they do that? Did they not learn from earlier experiences? I mean if you are an animal lover what do you shoot? Things like barn windows, friends, me, and the very, very worst, the whole interior of your bedroom. Ron loved tropical fish and had a huge aquarium in his room. One day, Mom and I heard a series of pings, glass breaking and water flowing. We entered the room to find Ron lying on the bed with his gun. He had shot out his window, the lamps, and the aquarium. When Mom questioned him as to why he would do such a thing his answer was truthful. "I don't know. I just couldn't help it."

We all worked together to get the fish in the bathtub and Mom started to clean. Bob, who was married at the time, came over to survey the damage with his sweet two-year-old daughter Kim in tow. No one was watching Kim who was watching the fish. Before we realized what was happening she had put Tide in the tub, had the toilet brush and was washing the fish. Dead fish. Nothing much came out of this. Ron was too old for the threat, "Do you want your spanking now or when you come home from school?" I remember how many times Mom repeated the aquarium story and the fake laughs she got from friends. They had to be wondering, what the hell was wrong with these people? Bob was probably thinking that if he had ever pulled such a stunt he would have ended up in the orphanage, a threat he heard often as a child when he didn't get his chores done.

Many years later, Bob had a little gun experience of his own. He and his wife Karen lived in an old rat infested house on the farm while building their home. One day he caught a giant rat in a garbage can in the house. He wasn't sure what to do with the rodent, so shot it with a German Lugar. Put a huge hole in the floor. Little animal, big gun. There was also the time that Ron and a buddy decided that they were going to be Mounties, but in order to do so you had to be able to ride. One morning they caught two gentle horses from the field and started riding up and down the fence line, talking about their futures as RCMP'S.

Bob looked out the window and just kind of wondered what would happen if he shot his shotgun into the air. Bang! The horses went straight up on their hind legs and the officers fell flat on their backs, the dreams of a future career over. Dad loved this story and his eyes would sparkle each time it was brought up.

A day perfect for hunting found Ron walking along Wellington Street with a rife slung over his shoulder. A police car stopped and Ron took off into the fields with the officer in pursuit. Mom was livid with the police department over this incident and she wouldn't let it go. Dad said it was no big deal, that she was embarrassing him by all the phone calls she was making to the Police Department, the Mayor, anyone that would listen. She wasn't mad at Ron. He was just walking along the road with a gun over his shoulder. She was mad at the officer who pulled his pistol on a twelve year old boy. Boys and their guns, just warms the heart!

ADULTHOOD

We three grew older, and left the nest . . . one flying free, the other two with a little nudge.

Our family became larger. Bob married Karen and had three kids-Kim, Bonnie and Robert. Karen was a hairdresser, which pleased Mom immensely. Not so much Karen. Mom could be a difficult client and would appear at the most inconvenient times for a perm. Dad offered to pay for a large wedding or give them a ten acre building lot. Bob jumped at the lot. I remember the day he left to get married. He kissed Mom goodbye and was gone. She immediately burst into huge, heart wrenching sobs and couldn't be consoled. I didn't know what to do so I just let her finish and go to the pantry under the pretense of making supper, but I suspect it was to just feel the loss of her eldest in private. Before she died Mom told me that her only regret in life was waiting too long to have another child after Bob.

Ron fell in love with Dixie when she was fourteen. Her family had come from Alberta but decided to go back. Ron at sixteen followed her out with some of his buddies. They took whatever jobs they could find. Both sets of parents finally threw in the towel and allowed them to be wed. Ron was nineteen, Dixie seventeen and after a short time they returned to Ontario. When they decided to go back out West in the summer of '71, we were all there as they pulled away from the farmhouse in their old Grand Prix, seats and roof spilling over with all the possessions they had in the world. They even had their old dog, Rufus, between them. Dad wept as he watched them leave. Ron and Dixie had three boys, Brad, and twins Mathew and Mark. They returned to Ontario after a couple of Alberta winters. These two women, Karen and Dixie, the wives of my brothers, became like sisters to me. We shared secrets, and private thoughts. I came to love them both dearly.

I met Ralph at Bob and Karen's one night while I was babysitting with a friend. We fell in love and were anxious to marry. The day finally arrived, September 4, 1965. My Mom wanted it to be a big wedding, me, not so much. The day that my Mother was picking out my wedding dress I went outside the store and sat on the steps of the salon. I'm told it was a beautiful wedding and everything went smoothly. I wasn't paying much attention. I was scared, shy and completely out of my comfort level. I just wanted it to be over so that Ralph and I could escape. The reception was winding down and my Father and I had our last dance. He began to sob so suddenly that I felt him buckle in my arms. I began crying and couldn't stop. Ralph and I were driving to visit with his family for our honeymoon and after several hours of my crying he finally asked if I wanted him to take me home. No, I was a married woman now, I had to grow up. Within a few short years I would be a mother to Kelly and Philip.

The day I married my relationship with my Father changed. We didn't belong to each other anymore. Even casual conversations stopped flowing and became strained. Mom and I grew closer and she was the only person on this earth who could make me laugh. One day we were shopping at Zellers and I was first at the checkout, with her just behind. I started putting my things on the conveyer belt and threw on an unfamiliar box. I didn't remember getting this. What was it? Condoms! She had thrown them in my basket when I wasn't looking. We both started to laugh so hard we couldn't stand up straight, and our lack of control felt so damn good. The cashier rolled her eyes and the people in line behind us started to tap their toes. This was the type of thing my Mother did. I once asked her, in all seriousness, if when she died she would leave me her sense of humor, her ability to laugh. She didn't.

I know that she was a little disappointed when she finally realized she would never have a prissy little girl whom she could adorn with ribbons and taffeta dresses. She'd had to settle for a wild child with filthy nails, smelling of horses, whose face and hair were usually dirty and legs and arms all scratched up from hay bales; a daughter who even licked the cow's salt block on occasion and could fight like a boy. On a trip to South America Mom bought me a painting that she said reminded her so much of me as a child that she couldn't resist buying it. Today that painting hangs directly in my line of vision when I sit in my chair. I stare at it often. It is all muted colors, greys and smoky blues. It shows a young girl surrounded by sand dunes looking out at the sea. She has on a long dress with a ribbon around the waist blowing gently in the breeze. She is holding a parasol. Not one strand of her long brown hair is out of place. I analyze it, too often, and it puzzles me. What part of me could she possibly see in that painting that would compel her to buy it, have it framed, and drag it all the way home from South America? Regardless, the two of us had fun, often under the disapproving eye of my Father.

CHAPTER II

A STORM LIKE NO OTHER

Ralph and I were just settling down to watch a movie when the call came. I remember being excited about the movie; it was one I was looking forward to seeing. I was just taking the pizza out of the oven when the phone rang. "Damn, it figures," I thought. It was Karen. She said she had bad news and I flippantly asked if her cat had run away again. "No" she replied "Your Mother has passed away. Your Dad found her on the bathroom floor." I now know what shock can do, how it protects your mind, actually takes away your thought process. I didn't ask how or when, I just murmured like a child, "What should I do?" She said to come.

It was a long, quiet drive. The sunset was unusually beautiful, all shades of pink, with little bits of red and blue. It was like some abstract painting. I watched the sky, inwardly calling out to her. "Where are you Mom, where have you gone?" In those hours, in my naivety, my first death, I thought there was no possible way on God's earth that she would leave me without giving some sort of sign, anything, to let me know that she wasn't just dead. Later I would really understand when people would say, "I can't believe he/she's gone," because they are just that, gone. No matter how much you wait, pretend and dream, you never hear from them again. I was jolted from my thoughts when I realized that Ralph was going the back way, the long way, with winding roads and tiny hamlets. Why wasn't he taking the main highway, the 401? I needed to get to my Dad. He explained later that he felt we were in no condition to be on the 401.

When we arrived Bob and Karen were there. Ron and Dixie had just gone home. Mathew, Ron and Dixie's son, and Deanna, who were to be married in two days' time, had driven from Guelph in the pouring rain. They looked shell shocked. I fell into my Dad's arms and found out what had happened. He'd found Mom by the toilet and had to pull her out by the feet so he could reach her to apply mouth to mouth. No man at eighty-eight years of age should ever have to try to revive his wife of nearly sixty-five years of marriage. It's just too sad. He said he knew she was gone the moment he touched her yet needed to try to bring her back to life. I felt such sorrow as I heard what had transpired that afternoon. Dad had managed to get Dixie on the phone and she was there in five minutes. He, in his sorrow, insisted that Dixie try mouth to mouth. Maybe he hadn't done it properly and there was still hope. She went through the motions for his sake, knowing it was far too late.

According to law because she died at home, police had to be called and there was a long wait for the coroner. I felt hurt for a while because they hadn't called me earlier, but after hearing how the scene played out I'm glad that they waited. Dad, of all people, knew how fragile I was. I could imagine him saying, "She doesn't need to see this." But still, when I allow myself to question it I find only confusion.

Matt and Deana were leaving to drive back to Guelph. Dad said it was too late for such a long drive and that they should stay. The thought flashed through my mind that even now, with numbness and confusion all around, that he was still thinking about the needs of other people. They insisted on leaving, probably to finally be able to cry in private. We went to bed and my only request was that Ralph and I sleep in my Mom's bed. After about an hour I heard a sound that made me feel as if my body was frozen, I really could not move. I was terrified. I had never heard such a sound before, bringing with it a feeling of sadness that went way, way down. It scared me, I was afraid my heart would stop. It was primal and my first thought was that an animal had been caught in a trap. It was my Dad. Bob got up and went to him. I heard quiet murmurs then there was silence for the rest of the night.

First we had the funeral parlor, then a wedding, then a funeral. Dad insisted on going to the wedding. It had been planned for two years, and it was family, his grandson. He was going to go only to the church ceremony but then decided to at least put in an appearance at the reception. Before we left for the church he called me into his room to ask if his tie and collar were right. As I reached to fix both I felt a little uncomfortable. I had never done anything like this for my Dad, Mom always had. Who would do it now?

It was such a beautiful wedding. Never have I seen a bride as radiant and happy as Deanna. There were few condolences, no mention that we had a funeral in two days. It was a celebration. I was reminded that the Burnett family crest says simply, 'Courage'. I snapped a picture that day of my Dad and Ron's three boys, Mathew the groom, Mark his twin and Brad the oldest. Mark is holding Brad's young son Kyle. Dad's face is a combination of pride and sadness. His strength shows through on the picture. It is one of the pictures that I cannot look at without tears.

Mom's funeral was nice. Even funerals can be beautiful in their way. She had prepared for this day by keeping a box full of instructions, poems, hymns and pictures. To her it would be the final social outing and she wanted it to be an event to remember. Things would have been so much easier if we could have found that bloody box. Every time Ralph and I would go to visit she would take me quietly into the bathroom where her jewelry was hidden in the shower, and go over it, piece by piece. She would show me all the appraisals, remind me which pieces were worth thousands and which were just eye-candy. With each piece there would be a story. Mom loved her jewelry. My eyes would glaze over and she would talk for what seemed like hours. It just all got so boring, she wasn't going to die anytime soon regardless of what she said. I would take care of everything. I never saw the jewelry. Poor lost Dad got all mixed up and gave Mom's costume pieces to family and her expensive gems to neighbors. So ladies, if you got a little 'reminder' of Helen in the days after her death, don't sell it at a garage sale!

I had also promised my Mom over and over again that she would have a closed casket. We had laughed often as she searched for that flattering, elusive picture to go on top of the casket. I made a vow to her that I would take care of things. The casket was open. I tried to explain to my Dad that she had requested a closed casket. His reply was that she thought she'd be old when she died, not young and still beautiful. She was eighty-three. I felt that I had betrayed her in so many ways; the open casket and not paying closer attention to the jewelry were the two that haunted me most. I had a lot of regrets and it had never, not once, entered my mind that I would. How can life take simple things like genuine promises and trust, and then carelessly throw them away? How can that be?

There was one piece of jewelry that missed the distribution. Just before she died Mom had bought a ruby and diamond bracelet. It still had the bill with it and she had paid thousands of dollars for it. Dad tried and tried to get his money back, and when he couldn't gave it to me. Meanwhile, Robyn, Philips oldest daughter had to write an essay in public school about a Canadian hero. She chose her grandfather. One of her paragraphs read "His dedication to his family and friends has served him well. He treats everyone he meets with the same soft spoken kindness, and is always the first to offer his help to those in need. Unlike most people, Stewart always prefers to help others anonymously, being more concerned with their needs than his own need to be acknowledged. He is one of the very few people on this planet who can honestly say" I've never met a person I didn't like." When I read this to Dad he started to cry and when he could compose himself he said, "You know that bracelet I gave you? When you are finished with it will you make sure that Robyn gets it?" So it waits for her.

We all wanted to know how Mom died, and when the report was available Bob went to the doctor to find out. She aspirated, choked on a teaspoon of peanut butter. She had been in one bedroom, Dad in another with the bathroom in between. They were both resting because they had to go out that night. She got up for some reason, and grabbed a spoonful of peanut butter, which she did often, then I guess, went to the bathroom. Bob asked the doctor if it was possible not to tell Dad how she had died. As Bob explained, Dad was hurting so badly he might get it in his head that he could have done something. The doctor said that by law he had to tell him if he asked. To his dying day, Dad maintained that Mom had died of a heart attack.

I stayed with Dad for a week after Mom died and it was hard, as if we were strangers with little to say to each other. The loss we saw mirrored in the other's eyes was a reflection of our own. We were just barely walking around, going through the motions. We were a reminder to each other of how much we loved and missed her. It wasn't working, so Karen, Dixie, Kim, Bonnie and I all took turns staying with him at night. When I was home again I missed Mom so badly that every day I wrote a phone conversation with her in a book. I told her all the news and gossip and she didn't need to reply because I knew exactly what she'd say. I heard it in my head. Make believe phone conversations; I did it for two years.

Dad stayed in the house alone during the day and one of us girls went down at night. Thankfully he had a lot of visitors. He was almost eighty-nine years old and Ralph and I started driving down from Brighton twice a week, then, as a bit of normalcy and routine gradually returned to his life, it became every Wednesday. We lived the furthest away and it took a total of five hours driving on the 401. I would often stay down for a few days. Ron and Dixie were only five minutes away and Bob and Karen about an hour. We all came, all of the family. Thank God my Father's cure for all things was work, the great healer. Work, church, his card group, the Lodge, his committees and friends—that's what got him out in the world.

CHAPTER III

CHANGES ON THE HORIZON

Ron and Dixie had a huge, rambling, century old, farm house in Zephyr. From the house there was a clear view of the barn and the cattle and horses grazing. It was an ideal place for Dad and Ron and Dixie wanted him there. Dad had an apartment built onto one end of the house. The construction was completed and Dad moved into his apartment in May of 2005. It was so perfect. He had a sitting room, a kitchenette, his own bathroom and a bedroom large enough to hold his giant desk. That desk was his private domain and we all felt as if we'd crossed some invisible line by just looking at it. The most appealing things about the apartment were the glass doors looking out to the barn and the wrap-around veranda. He even had his own exit where his car was parked so that he could come and go as he pleased. It was comfortable with a gas fireplace for winter nights. He ate all his meals with Ron and Dixie.

He befriended the two feral cats that would nervously follow him when he went to the barn. He'd count the cows every morning and night to make sure they were all there, and explained how he had to keep watch and count the pigeons because Ron was trying, unsuccessfully, to keep them out of the barn. He watched the cows and horses beginning and ending their day and the cats stalking a chipmunk; he knew which one was the lazy cat and which one the hunter. All of this he could see from his chair. He drove to church and meetings and often to Bobcaygen to have lunch with Bob and Karen. He went to auctions with Robert to buy cattle. Actually my Father seemed to have a multitude of lunch dates around this time.

There was always news when I called, and he seemed happy for the first time in a long while.

Every Wednesday when Ralph and I arrived for lunch and a visit, it would be the same routine. He'd be in his apartment with the door closed, waiting. We'd get a quick update from Ron and Dixie, about his health then I'd make a beeline to his apartment, a silly grin on my face, so glad to see him after a whole week. The others understood that I had to have my alone time with him first. I'd pop my head in and he'd grin and often say, "You're late." Sometimes he'd be watching Jerry Springer on television. A program he never imagined existed and believed to be true. That's the curse of the satellite dish. The others would join us shortly, thankfully, because Dad wasn't much of a talker. That's one thing I spent a great deal of time contemplating. He was so very, very quiet, how could he collect such a multitude of friends? Maybe it wasn't that he didn't talk much, perhaps it was just that he didn't talk unless there was something to say. He was comfortable with silence, not afraid of it and rushing to fill it with noise, like me.

We always ended up talking politics on our Wednesday visits, and the ridiculous decisions made by politicians and the justice system. He would tell us stories about when he was Reeve. On the larger political front, the letters N.D.P. would get Ron and I all worked up, and not in a good way. Dad would just watch us with affection. He was a staunch Liberal, as were the rest of the family until Harper came along, then we all defected. In local politics he often went for loyalty to a friend, rather than their party. Speaking of defecting, we teased him often about his backing of Belinda Stronach, and he always had the same answer, "She was a neighbor and a nice girl."

Our lunches were full of chatter, fun, good-natured teasing and lots of 'remember whens'. Wednesday become the highlight of my week, at least in the beginning. We'd laugh about episodes from the past, like the day Dad ran over Ron with the tractor. Ron was fine, but the mangled zipper on his pants showed how very lucky he was. "No wonder you got run over, you were always in the way. I'm surprised I only ran over you once." One afternoon Ralph and I and Ron and Dixie were complaining about our ages, what it's like not to be able to open jars, stiffness in the morning and the scary things that happen to your body that can convince you that you have some life threatening disease. Out of nowhere this quiet little voice said, "How would you like to be ninety-two?" We all felt a little humbled.

Dad told me that on Saturday nights he would have a shower and stand naked in front of the stove, drying in the heat, while he waited for the hockey game to come on television. I never told Ron and Dixie this for fear they'd never enter that room again on a Saturday night. Hockey Night in Canada; how long had it been part of our lives and the lives of our sons, grandsons and granddaughters? When we were little we always got a chocolate bar and a bottle of pop on Saturday night. Bob would head for his Popular Mechanics magazines, Ron and Dad would watch the game and Mom and I would sleep together in my bed. Ron and Dad would bunk down in the big bed after the game. Mom and I would hear them, farting and giggling through the night. It was all so peaceful and so very, very safe.

During the time Dad had his apartment with Ron and Dixie there was a serious power outage. It seemed to take ages to get the lights on again. It was especially slow in Zephyr and they went without electricity for three days. When your water comes from a well no hydro equals no water. One Wednesday just after things were back to normal, Dad mentioned that he had gone to church during this time. "How could you do that, you couldn't even wash?" I exclaimed, giving one of those looks of exasperation that you would give a child. "I washed with the water in the dehumidifier, it's new and the water was clean." Oh, right,

I never would have thought of that.

During another of our visits Dad told me he had fallen out of bed and given his head a terrible whack. I laughed and asked how he could fall out of bed. He had a good excuse, "Well, I usually get in on the side closest to the door, but for some reason I got in on the other side and when I went to roll over I fell out."

I could see no physical trauma at the time. I guess I didn't pay any attention. Why would I? Stuff like this happened all the time with Dad. Basically it was forgotten. I don't think he even told the others, I know I didn't. He had suffered a brain bleed and four fractured vertebrae in that fall from his bed, and life just went on as usual until the morning of March 16th when he didn't come out for breakfast. Finally at about ten Dixie went in and found him sitting in his chair surrounded by blood-filled tissues. He was coughing up blood and couldn't breathe. An ambulance was called and he was taken to the hospital where he was admitted as critical

My Father was confused, trying to get out of bed and didn't know us. He just starred off into space at a herd of cows, or a new gas station. I made him a little picture album of the family and horses and cattle to try to bring him back, but I don't think anything made sense to him at that time. I whispered memories hoping for some response. "Hey dad, remember the time you decided to get rid of the groundhogs and poured kerosene down the hole and lit it? It burned off your eyebrows and some of your hair. You had to go to Bob and Karen's to get some salve before you could go back to work. Remember?" He didn't respond. He was in the hospital for a week and finally got to leave when the pesky pneumonia had cleared up.

Pneumonia—the scourge of the elderly.

Around this time I started opening my mind, just a crack, to the fact that my father would die, probably sooner than later. Bob told me once that old age is like a terminal illness, no hope of a reprieve. I just didn't want to think about it, I was so afraid that when he did die I would be changed irrevocably and didn't know who I would be without him. He was my identity. That's who I was, that's all I was . . . . Stewart Burnett's daughter. Whenever I would tell people in the area my name the response would always be "Any relation to Stewart Burnett? Fine man, known him for years." One time I was actually approached by a stranger at a local event. She said to me, "You are Stewart Burnett's daughter aren't you? When I looked at your face I saw him."

He got better and was transferred to an independent living facility where he would have nursing staff on call yet be free to come and go. On the fourth day he called the nurse to say that he couldn't breathe. He was taken by ambulance to York County Hospital in Newmarket where he lay in emergency for twenty-four hours waiting for a bed. He had a clot in his lung that they were having trouble dissolving because he couldn't take blood thinners due to the old brain bleed. The first night on the floor he climbed over the rail of his bed and fell on his face. Dixie called me and told me to stay away for a few days; he just looked too bad and wouldn't know me anyway.

When we went the next day Dad looked like a defeated prize fighter. His head was cut open and still covered with dried blood. His eyes were black and swollen shut. His face was distorted and his nose wasn't where it was supposed to be. In his mind there was only one thing that he seemed to know for sure, he was on the farm and had work to do. My father didn't know who I was. The night before the nurses had tried to restrain him in bed, with disastrous results. He had gotten out of the restraints and broke a nurse's watch and ripped her uniform as they tried to tie him down. I didn't know this man.

It became obvious that he wasn't capable of independent living and the only solution was a nursing home. When we had discussed this possibility years ago, probably joking, not thinking it could ever happen to Dad, he had said that he wouldn't mind going into a nursing home as long as it was in Aurora so his friends could visit. We all felt lucky when we got the news that there was a vacant room, a private room, at the nursing home of his choice. This was good news because when you are on a waiting list you have to take whatever facility becomes available, or go to the bottom of the list.

The day Dad was to arrive at his new home, there was a mix up with ambulances, medical emergencies and his room wasn't ready. Ron was to meet him at the nursing home, but no one seemed to know where Dad was. He was 'on his way.' When he hadn't arrived by supper time Ron went home. He had waited all day and into the evening, but there were chores to be done and he had to eventually leave. I called the nursing home that night and Dad had arrived. My tears arrived about the same time. So, my Dad entered a nursing home, broken, bruised, alone, still confused, and still on the farm of his youth. I wanted him closer to Brighton, where we lived, but that's not what was best for him. I knew the bees would be buzzing. "Stewart is in a nursing home. Wouldn't you think that the family could take care of him instead of a nursing home? It's not that they can't afford it." They didn't know anything, nothing about what was happening, how we all felt, the hurt we had to endure to make that decision.

Fear started accompanying me on our Wednesday visits. My husband and children became second during this time. I could think of no one but my father. There was no need for apologies, my Father was dying and that had to be my main focus right now. If I had known that it was only the beginning of such a long journey, I would have asked for their forgiveness on bended knee.

When Dad entered the nursing home I decided to keep a diary. It maybe wasn't such a good idea when my Father's health began to deteriorate. If it was a bad, emotionally draining visit, I'd have to come home and re-live it as I put it on paper. It was difficult. It just got so hard to come up with one more word for pain, suffering, crying, loneliness, worry. When I decided to put my diaries in some kind of order, mainly for myself and my family, I wondered who would read my written thoughts, and what criticism would be expressed at the way I saw things, the way I felt, my need to express his pain. See, there it is again . . . . how many different words are there for pain? Many, and by the time I decided that I just couldn't do it anymore I had used them all up.

Dear Diary: May 2008

When Ralph and I walk through the door to my Father's new home for the first time, I find a lost little boy, quiet and unaware, not interested in anything we have to say. This is all so new to me, an uncharted land. I have never, ever seen my Father show his pain. No matter how bad one of his many accidents would be his medicine was always more work. It healed him.

Today for the very first time in my life, I see his pain, what it looks like. So horrible that it takes away all thought, even his willingness to speak. It renders him small, someone else, not my strong Father. His eyes are dull and he stares off into nothingness. What if he is captured in this state, never to return? I pray that he will drift off to sleep so that he can heal, however, when his eyes do close, thrashing, mumbling and twitching start; a nightmarish substitute for sleep. I hold his hand and stroke his hair. It surprises me how unlined his face is for a farmer who has worked out in the sun his whole life. It makes me question my hundred dollar face cream. I talk and talk, hoping for some reaction. My face close to his I whisper, "Remember when Mom made you go out east for a trip and you left Ralph in charge and a cow died, and, oh Dad, the time the boar gouged my pony's belly and we had to get the vet to sew her up? No wonder you didn't let us near the pigs." There is no glimmer of recognition in his eyes, except for a slight twinkle upon hearing the words cow and pony and boar, Things are happening on his own farm. He gives us no access, just smiles at things we cannot see. I'm curious as to where he has gone.

Dear Diary:

It is a happier visit today. He is less confused and no longer in as much pain. He still continues to stare, seemingly struggling to make out what he is seeing. Ralph and I are in his way, blocking his view. I try to look into his eyes to get his attention, but he just tilts his head to look around me. When we were children he would stand on the veranda with one hand shielding his eyes from the sun and look out across the fields. Searching for what? A cow down, a stray dog, or maybe he was just counting the herd. Is that what he is trying to do today? Maybe each time I speak he has to start counting all over again.

He is quiet but smiles more and the nurses give him a lot of attention. His needs are taken care of. When I tell a story about

Mom he gets a confused look on his face as if he doesn't know who I am talking about, and then the memory will return and he finishes the story with me. Quite often he drifts off to sleep and I watch him and just keep talking, hoping the sound of my voice will soothe him, like a verbal lullaby

The nurses tell me that he has started venturing from his room, greeting people that he's known from years ago, or their families, or the location of their old family homestead. He is adjusting, but still needs direction. He spends time in and out of reality. This just might be a good situation, he may enjoy the last years of his life. I tell him that it is a new beginning and that not many people get to start a new life well into their nineties. I wonder as we drive home if those were the right words. His reaction could easily have been "I'm in a nursing home; this is an end, not a beginning."

Dear Diary:

My optimism of last week leaves as I enter his room. His hair and shirt are drenched with sweat and he is pale with dark smudges under his eyes. He is so tired that he drifts off to sleep every time there is a break in the conversation. When he is awake he is still watching for something beyond the walls of this room. Could he be pondering his own death and deciding whether to come back or not. He seems to be so focused. "What are you looking at Dad?" "A herd of Belgium's" is his reply.

My Dad loved his Belgium's and his horses often won ribbons and trophies at all the local shows. In 1979 he won 'Best in Show Honors' at the Royal Agricultural Winter Fair in Toronto. His name is still well known among breeders in Canada and the United States. Belgium's are huge animals, usually gentle, but I, a lifetime rider, sometimes found myself a little bit intimidated by their size, their sheer volume. Mom was mad as hell at dad over an interview he gave to the paper about the horses. He said that they were all special, but that one called Betty would wink at him when he entered her stall. Mom was livid. She suggested that people would think him odd, and I guess a few did. Now I ask him if he remembers going to the doctors for a tetanus shot and telling the doctor that one of his horses had knocked him over while he was giving it a tetanus shot and the needle had gone through his hand. Would that count? The doctor said that would be fine. Hearing this brings a smile to his face and to mine.

He has a cough and chest congestion and no appetite. Maybe it's just the heat or he has a cold. It could even be that flu that's going around. On the plus side he gets up for meals and seems to be staying longer and longer in this time realm. Thank God for the nurses, they talk to him, tease him and are helping tremendously, they treat him with good natured humor, and often spend time in his room just talking.

Dear Diary:

Today, like a miracle, he is better. He has become so weak over the last few months that now he has started using a wheel chair. This surprises me a little. It seems that he began to use it, became dependent on it, in a very short time span, an indication of how tired he really is. He can't stand for long on his own. But his mind is again sharp, his humor intact. He tells us about going to a men's group, singing long-forgotten songs with others, and playing bingo. He is so very proud of the fact that he has physio on Thursdays and rides the exercise bike. The nurses walk with him every day, one holding each arm, and he counts how many lengths of the hall he can do.

Bob and Karen go to visit the next morning and he tells them, "It's a good thing the weather's bad because I was going to go on a boat cruise and would have missed you." Karen is the one who has to tell him that his older sister has just died. He says he'd better go to the funeral and that it was good she went fast. What will it be like tomorrow, the day of the funeral??

CHAPTER IV

ANOTHER FUNERAL

Why did I not know what an amazing woman my Aunt Agnes was? Agnes was Dad's older sister, a woman I was frightened of as a child. She adored Bob and it was mutual. Ron and I were not her favorites. She wouldn't hesitate to give us a good 'crack in the lug' if she felt it necessary. She lived with our grandparents, looked after them until their deaths. She was a stern Scottish matriarch, quiet like Dad, with no time for nonsense, and no patience for kids that didn't know their place. Her bedroom at the top of the stairs was like a shrine and, although Ron and I were curious we would never go in. The door was always open and when we had to go past the room we ran. It seemed to call to us to enter, like the Sirens of Mythology. Everyone at the funeral parlor was waiting for Dad, wondering if he would come, wondering if he should, or more precisely if he could. Then he made his entrance, head weaving from side to side so that he wouldn't miss contact with anyone. Ron wheeled him to the casket and I felt such a rush of tenderness for my brother. It was as it should be. After saying goodbye to his sister, Dad went visiting. I thought he looked very delicate-then I changed my mind-his body is frail, the man is steel.

The service started and two women clinging to each other for support began speaking about how Agnes took over after their father, Dad's brother Norman, died leaving four children under the age of four, (it was Norman that Dad would be working with when he went to the farm of his childhood in his mind).

I sat there fascinated; listening to my two cousin's talk about a woman I saw every Sunday as a child and didn't even know. They obviously loved her very, very much.

Agnes never married and Norman's widow, Aunt Margaret and the children became her family. She would take the kids and any friends that were around on outings. She always had a tin of salmon sandwiches. Agnes was famous for her salmon sandwiches. She went to every hockey game the twins, Jim and John, played in, and brought cans of pop when they practiced on the pond. Agnes was there through tears and joy, weddings and funerals. As I listened to these two women, and saw the pain etched on their faces, I finally understood that I had missed out on something that I would never be able to have.

She was probably the only business owning woman in Richmond Hill, at a time when women hadn't even thought about going to work. She had her own insurance company and she was the one Dad went to when he and Mom bought their first new car. They couldn't understand this charge they called 'interest'. Dad was incensed when Agnes explained it all to him and vowed he would never, ever pay another cent of interest for the rest of his days. She lived and died on her own terms. What a remarkable, courageous woman. The Minister spoke of Agnes and her life. At one point he said please stand. I glanced at Dad sitting in the aisle in his wheel chair and all seemed well until his hands went to the arms of his chair and he gathered all his strength and got to his feet, swaying from side to side ever so slightly. The Minister, about to start the prayer, bowed his head. Dad's youngest sister Mary was telling him to sit down before he fell down. We all rushed to him saying, "Dad, sit down." and he said "The Minister said to stand." Karen was urging Bob to 'do something'. The Minister was waiting to continue. Dixie positioned herself behind the wheelchair with her hand on Dad's shoulder. This was a prayer with eyes wide open, except for my father who was standing tall with head bowed and eyes closed. I just stood watching, not even attempting to pray. I couldn't make up my mind whether to laugh or cry and the only person that knew what to do was my Father.

Getting the wheel chair to the grave site, over mud, grass, sod and tarp was a struggle with everyone participating. Dad had to be almost carried as the wheels of the chair kept getting bogged down in the mud. Bob and Robert were trying to wheel it with Dad's heels digging into the ground, until Dixie finally took hold of his pant cuffs and held his feet up. I held the umbrella over us all. After the short message at the grave the Minister finally said that Agnes would want us to leave, to go home out of the rain.

Then the Minister said, "I have to see this guy", and he came over to Dad and spoke to him with genuine affection. He told him that he looked well and Dad replied, "I'll be 84 in September" and I said "94" and the Minister, in mock horror, replied "Lying to a Minister Stew, that's really bad." Laughter bubbled up in Dad, pure joy, the kind of joy that we younger, busier people, struggling with all the wrong things, hardly ever get to feel.

Later on Dad was sitting in the car with the door open and I went to say goodbye. Finally the tears pooled in his eyes. He told me that he had wanted to go to the far lengths of the cemetery to see the graves of his parents and grand-parents. It was too wet, and he'd left it too late. I made myself a promise that one day I'd go back to that cemetery behind the church in Richmond Hill. I wanted to see all the family graves of those brave people who came to a new land to clear the bush and build their lives. I added it to my 'bucket list'. We talked about the coming week, if Wednesday was still a good day to visit or if his busy schedule warranted a change. I kissed my Father. I kissed my brothers, sisters, all the rest and left, slightly changed and slightly altered. Agnes was 97 and had been living in her own apartment when she passed away.

Dear Diary:

There is no warning sign on the front door of the nursing home yet it turns out the second floor is under quarantine. We didn't even realize that Dad was in isolation until they brought his lunch to his room. The whole floor is off limits to visitors; at least it's supposed to be. Today he has no voice and a sore throat. It is obvious that he feels too tired and sick to participate in any sort of dialogue. I ask the nurse to check him and she tells me that the doctor has already ordered blood work.

I wonder what story from days gone by will cheer him up and remember Pearle Hale. Pearle used to come to visit on the old farm, the Preston farm. All three of us kids were positive that she was a witch, and she looked the part; old, wizened, hunched over, wearing long layers of dresses, and a shawl, walking with a cane. We would shutter if we saw her heading up the long lane towards the house. Hide! Once she loaned me a book. It must have been for Mom to read to me because it was long before I could read by myself. I was so afraid something would happen to that book and it did. Ron scribbled all over the inside covers with lipstick. He was very young at the time, but why did it have to be that book! It was a horrible situation and I cried during the day and had nightmares at night. No words of comfort from my parents could calm me. Mom tried to fix the book by pasting the blank pages together. It looked almost brand new, she said, but not to my eyes. Today Dad finishes the story for me. "And one day when she was coming up the lane Rusty knocked her over and broke her leg." No worries about the book, she never came back. Maybe she died, maybe our dog killed old witch Hale.

Ron popped in while we were there and Dad's favorite nurse came in for a quick visit. The summer Olympics were on television and Eric Lamaze was riding for gold. My eyes were glued to the television. It puzzled me that no one in that room seemed to care when he won gold. I was ecstatic. I guess one reason was that Ralph, Ron and Dad were talking hockey. The nurse and I began talking about Cuba. I glanced at my Father often and put my hand on his arm to remind him that we hadn't forgotten about him. He just seemed content to lie there and watch us, to listen to us ramble on, like the old days. He was upbeat when we left, planning his day and evening.

Ron and Dixie usually went to see Dad on Tuesday, Ralph and I on Wednesday and Bob and Karen on Thursday. We never got to be together to chat and laugh and enjoy each other anymore. I missed it. If Ralph and I were going to drive such a long distance, it had to be to see dad. We six couldn't afford the luxury of visiting each other at this time. But, there were a lot of phone calls, and lots and lots of e-mails.

Dear Diary:

From one Wednesday to the next, in one short week, I can get lulled into a false security about my Father; forget that he has a cancer that has spread throughout his body. One brother says he's getting better not worse and so it seems. He is grinning when we arrive today and when I ask him what is so funny he says he was thinking about the time he took Ron and me to the general store to buy sausages. "Big as your thumb and all attached." He'd bought the sausages, put them and us in the car and went back into the store to chat. When he came out we had taken the sausages out of the pink colored butcher paper, rolled down the window and were dangling them up and down outside the car as if we were fishing. "But Dad," I tell him, "We were fishing." We laugh and gossip and it is so good. He didn`t doze off once and there were no lulls in the conversation. I, for the first time ever, am not watching the clock, trying to think of ways to fill the silences. We began talking about cemetery plots-mine and Ralphs-and then cremation and he said something that touched me deeply. He said, "If you are being cremated then the kids could bring some of your ashes down and put them with your mother and me." Me. He said that to me. It was a gift that left me momentarily speechless. As an adult, I had often felt unworthy; as if I didn't deserve this wonderful life I'd been given.

That was this week what will next week bring? Mountains and valleys. Get to the top and think you are, for a little while, safe from sorrow, and then Dad slips and pulls you down the slope leaving you wondering if you can climb it again. Anyway, today was the best.

Dear Diary:

Today we 'shot the breeze' as they say. He is glad to see us but conversation is limited. He is feeling kind of blah. He doesn't even feel up to teasing Ralph, one of the things he truly enjoys. He had a lot of visitors last week, three times on Monday alone, and I selfishly wish so many people wouldn't come. They bring in tons of food which bothers him because he knows he won't eat it all and doesn't want to be wasteful. I'm the one who has to tidy it all up, organize his fridge, and get rid of what he doesn't want. I should rephrase that, I'm not the one that has to do it, to do anything when we go to visit. It's just that I feel a need for order in his room, in his life.

Nursing home rooms are small and sterile looking, no different than a hospital room. We all tried to make his room as much like home as possible when he moved in, but his own bulky furniture just wouldn't fit. His huge desk remained in his bedroom at Ron and Dixie's. We did manage to get his favorite chair in, thank God, because Dad had a long history of good and bad chairs. We hung one of his paintings of a team of white horses pulling a wagon across a stream. It had been in the house for years, I think he bought it at a farm auction. He would say that they were his horses, I think just to make Mom mad, and mad she would get. She would try to reason with him but was wasting her words. Another case of, "Stewart, people are going to think there's something wrong with you." He didn't care, just kept maintaining they were his. Karen and Dixie bought him sheets which he immediately dismissed as too hot. Bob and Karen got him a television and a bar fridge that he could get to with his wheel chair. There were pictures from great-grandchildren on the walls and plants on the window sill. We all tried to take away the sparseness and somehow make a nursing home room a home. He assured us that he didn't mind if the room was lacking in 'things'. He had all that he needed. Besides, too much stuff just got in the way of the wheelchair.

Mom often called Dad cheap, and said he was 'tighter than bark to a tree'. And he was tight with a dollar, yet he was the most generous man I ever knew, as long as it was important and made your life better.

He used to show up at Bob and Karen's every Saturday morning, no knock, just two sharp kicks to the door to let them know he was there. He would have a coffee and a short visit and then be off to look for work to do. One day he showed up wearing one black shoe and one brown shoe. When Bob questioned him he said simply that one had worn out. And ever the thrifty one, he had his false teeth for over seventy years. When they would get a sharp edge on them he would take them to the garage and grind them down with the grinder. It's strange when I think about it, but not once as a child did I see him without those teeth in his mouth. I was shocked in later years when he took to wiggling them around to traumatize a grandchild.

The joy and excitement of buying a new car was over-shadowed by the fact that we would, eventually, have to tell Dad, and it would always be the same refrain. "What's wrong with the old one, still runs good doesn't it? And if you finance it and pay interest you need your head read." That was always one of Dad's favorite sayings. You need your head read. Bob didn't care what Dad thought about buying a car, he was defiant, if he wanted a car he'd just buy it, and then with a grin say, "Bought a vintage Corvette the other day." Dad would never question what he did, just shake his head.

When Bob bought a new Harley Davidson motorcycle, Dad had just had a car accident that resulted in a cast from his ankle to his groin. Although he was a little hesitant, Bob talked him into taking a spin on the bike. It was hard to position the cast so Bob put it on his lap. We were all there to see the new motorcycle, but somewhat skeptical about Dad getting on with his cast. It was such a huge, powerful machine. To show just how powerful the bike was Bob took off at a tremendous speed and dad went flat out backwards just like a human board. The only thing that kept him on the bike was Bob's strong grip on his foot.

The cast was the result of Mom and Dad's first car accident. They had others and hit a deer twice. This time the doctor said his knee damage was similar to taking a hammer to an egg shell and steel pins had to be put in to try to put the knee back together. Of course Dad continued to do the chores and clean out the pigs and when he finally went to the hospital to have the cast removed so much pig manure came out that they had to move to another room while the staff tried to clean the original one. The smell was the worst part. Mom was very, very angry.

We didn't go down this Wednesday because Dad was going on a field trip to a farm. I called that night to see how the outing had gone. He was quite peeved. Seems the farm had visited them with a calf and a goat and a pony. He was disappointed, had been looking forward to being in a barn again, and talking with the farmer. What do you want to bet that it would be someone he knew? Not a possibility but a probability.

Dear Diary:

Dixie phoned to tell me that he fell and had to go to the hospital again. He'd had a dream that the cattle were out and had climbed out the end of the bed, tripped over the chair and fell. When we get to the hospital we are again strangers to him. He is picking at the bed clothes, trying to get out, talking about things that make no sense at all. He is back in that nightmarish place he always enters when he passes through the doors of a hospital. He is lost in some sort of Hell. He finally makes it back to the nursing home, confined to bed, being fed in his room, still not knowing where he is.

Dear Diary:

Today shows me that maybe I worry too much (what a surprise). He is back to normal; happy, alert and interested in his surroundings. As I write this the thought flies through my mind "Is this his normal now?" He has grown more and more content in the nursing home. He is preoccupied by the comings and goings of the institution. In the middle of any conversation if he hears voices outside the room his attention is immediately diverted to the door. He likes to know what's going on. It's become his community.

I was so scared when I heard that he'd had another fall that I went in and gave him proper hell. Dad puckers his lips sometimes when he feels emotion. He kept looking at Ralph and shaking his head, as if it was funny that I was so upset, but at one point he looked as if he might cry. How cruel of me to remind him that he can't stand up anymore, that he needs help to even get into his chair. He'd had a dream that took him back to when he was younger and stronger. Damn, I just can't seem to do anything right. He had a little box of candy waiting on his table for me that he had won at bingo. Dear sweet Dad I'm so sorry.

There was a special anniversary service at his little church, Wesley United, and he wanted to go. We just didn't know whether this was a good idea. As the weeks had turned into months, he had stopped wanting to leave the comfort of the home, even for a drive, saying it was too much trouble. It was hard, due to the fact that he couldn't sit longer than fifteen minutes without pain setting in. But in this case I guess he just wanted to see his beloved church and old friends one more time. The church has steep, wide stairs inside, and there are always a lot of people milling about. Ron and Dixie took him, and there was the problem of how to carry the wheelchair, with him in it, up the stairs. He insisted on getting out of the chair and with Dixie on one side and the sturdy hand rail on the other slowly began making his way up. He fell at the top of the stairs and had to be helped up by old, yet young, friends. He couldn't sit in the hard pews but wouldn't sit in the aisle and 'block traffic'. He got confused and agitated and cried, in front of all his friends. I cannot for one moment fathom the sadness and humiliation he felt. He showed everyone at that church what he didn't ever want them to see.

What a part that church played in our lives. Mom singing in the choir, which at times could be pretty brutal because there were only about eight members and they often didn't know the hymns very well. Dad always sat in the same pew, same spot, grinning each time a person would stop to talk or just give the farmer's nod of greeting.

We used to tease him because he never sang the hymns, just moved his lips.

It was an old church, even then, with wooden floors that sloped towards the front. Susan and I used to drop pennies during the service and listen to see it they rolled all the way to the front. On the wall hung the magnificent chimes that my mother's mother had donated to the church. They weren't played often, but when they were the sound was so beautiful, it gave the whole church an extra feeling of reverence, as if angels could descend at any time. The stained glass windows were bright and colorful and during a boring service (which they all were for children) I would lose myself in them. Each one told a story from the Bible.

Sunday school, Bible Study, Summer Camp, Christmas Concerts, and Bazaars; so much revolved around that little church on the corner. I was baptized and married there. When we six had to start talking about Dad's funeral we knew that he had always said he wanted it to be at the church. We wondered whether we could get a casket through the door. Bob said that if that's what Dad wanted we'd get the casket through even if we had to take all the doors off the church. Dad never mentioned his church visit, nor did I.

Dear Diary:

When we walk in today and he smiles and says "Well look who's here" I feel such love, mixed with relief that it's going to be a good day. Then he tells us that he just walked to the bathroom on his own, and it mystifies me, because I know he can't, yet somehow can, and does so on occasion. He talks about his lone treks to the bathroom with pride. Today he seems to be a much younger man. He is curious about the weather. When his whole life has depended on the elements he must yearn to feel the wind on his face, yet he won't let me take him outside, and I will not force him with words of how good it would be for him. My thoughts are not his. There's a woman across the hall who screams all the time and he tells us that she's calm when he talks to her. She's taken to coming into his room at night, and one night he woke up with her trying to get in bed with him. After our jokes and laughter he grumbled that he has to shut the door at night now and doesn't like to because then he can't see what's going on.

A huge part of his day seems to be spent watching the black squirrel that lives outside his window and every week he has an update on that squirrel, also the cats at the Day Care Center that come out at the same time every day to look for mice. And, he talks about all the crows, how loud they are and how busy.

"You and Ron used to catch crows and put them in the milk house. There were all these crows."

No Dad, they weren't crows, they were pigeons. The ingenious process of catching those birds comes rushing back and again it makes me thank God for the life this man has given us. Ron and I came up with some pretty good ideas, but the pigeon one was sheer genius. Around dusk, in the summer months, we'd set out across fields carrying a bag and a flashlight heading out to barns within the area. Pigeons roost at night, go to sleep, and in a barn there is usually a light just inside the door. It was all so simple. Find a barn, find the light, and give it a quick switch on to check to see if there are any pigeons and if so where. Then one of us would stay by the light and the other would start climbing old rickety wooden ladders to the second story of the barn. Flick the light on/off, shimmy across a bean towards an unsuspecting pigeon, flick, closer, then grab the pigeon and put it in the bag. It worked so well. If I were the climber my greatest fear wasn't falling, we'd passed that one a long time ago, but putting my hand on a snake on one of the beams, and there was always the fear, the deep fear of getting caught by an angry farmer. Walking home in the dark, through unfamiliar fields, carrying our bag, there was always the chance of stepping on something, or falling in a hole. The worst part was what could be behind us, following us. It could be a crazed farm owner, a wild animal, or even a ghost. The walk home was the scariest part of the whole endeavor. We'd drop the pigeons off in the milk house with the others and run to the warmth and safety of our home. "Where were you two?" Mom would ask," I was getting worried." Catching pigeons we'd tell her. The only comment Dad ever made was to 'get those damn birds out of the milk house'. Today his comment is "Never any eggs. You would think that with all those pigeons there would be eggs."

I took in a small piece of my philodendron, one of those long green leafed jungle plants that grow like a vine, to put on his shelf and it amazes him how fast it grows. In a short space of time it has almost reached the floor. Dad says that it only gets watered and taken care of on Wednesdays. A little thing like a plant with all the turmoil of a nursing home caught up in its fragile leaves, doing its part—trying to add a little beauty to the world. Now it is back where it started, on a bookcase in our home, still thriving without much care. Philip has a piece he calls 'Stewie" and each time he looks at it, or waters it, he thinks of his grandfather.

Dear Diary:

No trucks on the 401 today! Dad is just getting out of bed without any help when we arrive. He says he heard us coming and wanted to get into the wheelchair. I give up. If a fall is what takes him so be it. He seems mentally and physically fine. When I ask him if there are any new scandals his eyes light up and he tells a story about a woman at his and Walt's table who got fed up at Walt's sexual remarks and asked to be moved. Dad has known Walt for his entire adult life. He's a good friend, but can be a little raunchy. Can't help but laugh at his crude jokes. I think that's one of the things Dad likes about Walt. He is comical.

He also tells us about a dream he had the other night. He was at Ron's farm, drawing in hay. He climbed out of bed, dreaming that he was climbing off the tractor and proceeded to move his bed around the room thinking it was the hay wagon. A nurse came in (he has one of those alarms that buzzes at the nurse's station when he gets out of bed) and told him that if he got out of bed again she'd tie him in. He said he told her it was just a dream and got back into bed, he also said he told her to find another job, one that she was good at. Although at the time we laughed at his audacity, it surprises me, worries me. Dad is never cruel to anyone, especially the nurses (hospital stays don't count). What had happened to make him react that way? I chewed on it all week and different scenarios would emerge in my mind. I began to wonder about things that happen that we never hear about. Had she been cruel? Hurt him putting him back to bed? Maybe it was the threat to tie him in that did it, bringing back memories of the hospital. But they know, all of the nurses, that if he were abused in any way he'd tell us. Or would he?

The thought of him saying that to a nurse made me think about the worm pickers and how his temper flared over what he saw as an injustice, the breach of a promise. He was approached by an Italian group that asked if they could pick worms from one of his fields. They would pay him a small fee, so of course Dad said yes. They would show up at dusk, men and women with lights attached to their heads, and all night would walk up and down the fields looking for night crawlers. In the morning they would gather between the two barns and the women would make breakfast. It was rather unsettling to see them squatting around fires, like gypsies. We three kids didn't like it; the thought of Mom and Dad sleeping with doors unlocked while total strangers prowled around, but dad said they weren't doing any harm and seemed like friendly people.

He changed his mind one evening when he and a friend were coming home from a Lodge meeting and he spotted the lights in a field he had just ploughed, a field they had no business being in. Dad was crazy with anger. He was a fair age at this time, as was his friend. They rushed home to get Ralph and headed out to the field. I guess Ralph was to be their protector in case things got out of hand. There was a lot of shouting between Dad and a young man who had a pail of worms in each hand. Without warning Dad raised his boot and kicked the pails from his hands. Worms were everywhere, even in the man's hair and on his shoulders and dangling from his ears like earrings. Now Ralph thought "Oh great, all of them, two old men and me." He told me later that he thought that they were afraid of dad and suddenly became extremely polite, offering to leave right away. They never came back, but I'm sure that during quiet times over coffee and cigarettes they still talk about that Stewart Burnett. Crazy. Dad would not tolerate being cheated or lied to.

When Mom died Dad had thirty cattle. These weren't stabled like the early years. They wintered in a huge, open area in one of the old barns on the property and could go in and out freely, but the manure still had to be cleaned out and they had to be fed all winter. Then summer would come and the cattle would want greener pastures. Dad would often get a call in the middle of the night saying that his cattle were out on Wellington Street. Up he'd get and go out in the dark alone to gather them all up, find a gate, or the broken fence and get them back into the field. This seemed impossible in the pitch black of night. Speeding cars often couldn't see the cows, just this very old man emerging from the ditch. Many times the call would go to Ron. Everyone knew whose cows they were. "Stew Burnett's cattle are on the road again. Better get Ron out here." And that would be the police.

We six worried about him, but also felt a little angry when he would tell us about a knock on the door from a stranger in the middle of the night to say that cattle were on the road. Why did he have to have those cattle in the first place? The answer was so obvious that it just added to the frustration and worry. When would it ever end? We used to grumble about how a man who was constantly fixing fences could have so many escapees. One day I asked him why he kept the thirty cattle when they were so much work and the profit couldn't be very high. "Well", he said "By the time I subtract the cost of hay, straw and vet, I figure I can make two thousand dollars in a year." I couldn't believe what I was hearing. All that work for a measly two thousand dollars?

Dear Diary:

He is sleeping when we arrive. I just stand by his bed for a few moments and wait for him to open his eyes. When he is not in distress I enjoy watching him. It calms me and I get so much pleasure out of just remembering. When he is finally awake I ask him how he is getting along with the nurse he had chewed out. "Good, good, she just needed to be told. We're friends now." I still wonder what happened, what she said or did to him, but I guess he handled it the way he always does and made a friend in the process . . . . unlike the worm pickers. When he falls back to sleep I clean his closet and find a lot of his next door neighbor's clothes. The neighbor died last week.

As I was rushing around cleaning his closet and fridge and watering his plant, I did a terrible thing, the very worst thing I could do. I upset the candy jar. This particular candy jar wasn't even a jar, but a big plastic jug and it always had to be full because it was for the nurses. I brought candy every Wednesday and one week I didn't bother because the week before I had filled it to the brim and even put some extra in his drawer. I thought there would be enough for at least two weeks. When we got there it was less than half full. That container couldn't ever be empty. The nurses (and one verified this) hide in his room, just for a little break, some conversation and to eat candy. I had to call Dixie that night to go and get candy in the morning.

An hour's visit is all that Dad can take so we are back on the road at noon, stop for a burger, pick up the dog at the kennel, and get home around four. I can't believe that we have been making these Wednesday trips for eight years. How can that possibly be? They started when my Mom died, continued throughout his stay at Ron and Dixie's and now each week to the nursing home. For eight years we've fought our way through all of the elements, but, the most dangerous, worse than Mother Nature herself, are the trucks on the 401. When there are a lot and they seem unusually reckless the thought always creeps into my mind that we shouldn't be there. I wonder how long it will continue. Part of me says 'I'm tired', the part of me where my heart lives says, "We can do it. I hope it goes on for years." Sometimes it's a fun outing and sometimes I cry or just stare out the window. It all depends on how Dad is.

Dear Diary:

Today he wants to talk to the doctor about sweats that he gets daily; sweats that leave his shirts drenched and keep him awake at night. The doctor comes in and says it is probably from the cancer, or medication, but that he'll order tests just to be sure. I follow him out into the hall and tell him that I've noticed Dad's speech has been a little slurred the last couple of weeks. He asks if I think the cancer has reached the brain, and should he order a cat scan. I wonder why he is asking me, but say no, it isn't that bad yet.

It's a cool, overcast day and dad's mood matches the weather. He is fed up. I remind him that he has had worse days, for example the de-horning incident that took place years ago.

The minute I begin, with input from Ralph, Dad's face changes. The sadness leaves his eyes and he forgets about his pain. Dehorning cattle is the most violent job on the farm. It is bloody and dangerous. Cattle bawling as they rub their now hornless heads against the barn, eyes full of fear, blood shooting out of the cavity where the horn used to be, like a severed artery. It really is like a war zone. Dehorners resemble huge garden shears, each arm about four feet long with curved cutters on the end.

On this day Dad was struggling to hold a crazed cow around the neck while Bob and Ralph (two unlikely candidates) each had one handle of the dehorner. The terrified cow twisted just as Dad yelled 'pull' and when the horn snapped off dad had his elbow caught in the gears of the dehorner. He turned white and fell to his knees, but didn't pass out and wouldn't go to the hospital. Later Karen went out to the field, got him off the tractor and made him go. The story cheers him, the long forgotten pain somehow negating the pain he is feeling now. And it always makes me laugh to hear him blame others for his mishaps, in this case Bob and Ralph. If another person is involved in one of his accidents, it's always, in his mind, their shortcomings that caused the whole thing.

As I snuggle in to him to say goodbye he whispers in my ear "Be kind to each other, one day one of you will be gone." His words startle me because of the truth behind them. One day one of us will be gone, with no second chances. Loneliness.

I speak to the nurses about his condition and tell them that if he asks a question to please be truthful with him. Liza in particular seems to care about his well-being and promises that she will contact me if he needs me to come or if his condition changes. We exchange e-mail addresses. She tells me that she was immediately drawn to him when he first arrived at the home, battered and bruised. She thinks it was his quiet, kind demeanor, and says that she has never felt that way about a resident in the many years she has worked at the home. She hugs and kisses him often. It relieves my worries a bit to know that I have someone there watching out for him. Dad asks me to bring in a little something for Liza to thank her for all her kindness. I question in my mind how a mere box of chocolates can show the gratitude I feel.

Dear Diary:

I got home Monday from a well needed vacation. On the way to Aurora I wonder what I will find after three weeks away. My heart melts a little bit. He looks like Alfalfa from the Little Rascals television program. His hair is all messed up because it needs cutting and he is out of Brylcreem again. Bloody Brylcreem. Better remember to add it to the list.

He is excited and waiting to tell us that he is about to receive his fifty year pin from the Masons. Dad has obviously been a Mason for most of my life. Bob too. Mom, Karen and I used to spend hours speculating as to what went on at the meetings. And what was the meaning of those aprons that they wore? Why was it such a secret? Why were women banned? I decide that today is the day to share a secret the women of the family have been keeping for years. Nights when he and Bob would be at their Masonic meetings, we women would all meet at Karen's house to take part in the popular, but illegal pyramid schemes. Every now and then Mom would laugh and wonder what Dad would say if he found out, especially since he was Reeve at the time. It would definitely cause a scandal. Now he just gives a couple of tsk tsks's and shakes his head, looking at Ralph for agreement. "See" I smile, "You had your little secrets, but so did we." I laugh at the look on his face, the ridiculousness of it all so typical of our family.

He sleeps, plays Bingo and waits for his family, Ron popping in before hockey, grand-daughters coming in every week, Kim to bring food to encourage his eating and to cut his hair, Bonnie bringing boxes and boxes of food and clothes, Robert wanting to know what to do with a sick cow, Bob and Karen dropping in on their way home from Toronto, Dixie stopping in whenever she is in town, Mark telling him stories about his daily life as a police officer, Mathew running in on weekends when he has a few moments from his high pressure job and quiet Brad to talk about the building boom and how it affects his business. And, without fail, our Wednesday visits. Mark tells the stories dad remembers most, the ones he relishes. He listens so intently that he almost forgets to breathe. And when Mark goes to visit him in uniform he can hardly contain his pride, suggesting that Mark take him around for a little ride in his wheelchair for all to see.

One of Dad's proudest moments was the time he sold a horse to the Metro Police Department. I remember the day they came to pick it up. I watched as Dad and the officers tried to load a frightened, young horse into their van. It took hours and I marveled at their professionalism, combined with Dad's experience. Finally Dad suggested that they put the horse in the barn, back the van up to the door and lead her from the darkness of the barn into the trailer. Worked like a charm. It took them almost all afternoon and I have never seen such gentle, patient handling of a horse. Their main focus seemed to be to keep her calm and not use force of any kind. I was impressed. Dad kept tabs on the horse and they sent pictures occasionally. If he would see mounted officers on television he would say, "There's the horse I sold to the police department." I used to think, "Right Dad, like the picture of the team crossing the stream in the old painting." However, with my Father, you never knew for sure. He knew his horses.

It's true, what goes around comes around. We aren't the only lucky ones, he is too, because he has us and lord how we've worried about him over the years.

Stewart's many accidents became legendary throughout the community. Some people even looked for unworldly reasons why he was still alive. They started decades ago and never let up. He really did have more lives than a cat, several cats. He once fell out of an apple tree with a running chain saw. He told us that he met one of the women from the church and when she asked about the scratches on his face he told her the story. Her reply was "What the hell was an old man in his eighties doing up a tree in the first place?" That same year he was hammering fence posts when the head came off the hammer hitting him in the face and breaking his nose. He used both hands to crack his nose back into place and continued working. His shirt was so bloody it had to be thrown out. One sunny Sunday in December the grandchildren wanted to play hockey on the pond but it was covered with snow. Dad said that was no problem but it quickly turned into a disaster. The kids couldn't really use the whole pond for their hockey game because there was a huge hole gushing water where the tractor went through the ice. Upset tractors rolling down hills, car accidents, bites from boars that torn his pants from his body, being knocked unconscious by a horse, falling from the house roof, going through the barn floor spread eagle, so he couldn't move up or down. Accidents became comical after the fact, but I often shook my head in despair at this exasperating, stubborn man. Another accident that caused a great deal of worry was when he was combining a field (cutting and retrieving the oats or wheat), and a chain came loose on the combine. He had his hand right in the grinding part of the machine and somehow got it caught. By the time he had disengaged himself his hand was mangled and bleeding. He arrived at Bob and Karen's asking for a darning needle and black thread and proceeded to sew it up so he could get back to the field.

My Father took a lot of pride in his home remedies and often sewed up a wound. There was something rather unsettling about watching him, hunched over and concentrating hard, sewing up his own torn flesh. When as adults, we would go to visit, he would show us a new 'battle scar', and assure us that there was no need to go to the hospital, he'd just put some Vaseline on it. For muscle pain he used an inordinate amount of WD-40 from the hardware store. Mom remarked once that she had never seen a person heal as quickly as Stewart. Thank God. This is one time he can't just forget about the pain, can't fix himself from his little bag of tricks.

The C word. He and I can now bring it out into the light, talk about it. We talk often about his prognosis and he asks me questions. The cancer needs to be talked about, but it gives me such a feeling of dread that if it were possible I'd deny its existence, but he's too smart for that and I have to prepare for the deadly invasion, so that I can be there for him. The one thing I don't know, the one thought that ravages my mind is not that he is going to die, but how will it be? Every single time we arrive at the home I am brimming with excitement to see my Dad, but full of uncertainty as to what I'll find when I walk through that door. It's like a foreboding voice in my head. If Dad's well, the voice disappears, if not it stays, becoming louder and louder and interfering with my thoughts. It's only refrain during bad times is "Your Fathers going to die, your Dad will soon be dead, and then what will you do?"

Ralph says little, especially when Dad's bad, but he watches every move I make, tries to judge how emotionally stable I am feeling. He feels impotent to say or do anything, knowing that the wrong words can send me spiraling into depression or anger. He thinks I have had enough and shouldn't go to Aurora as often, but he is powerless to stop me. Ralph loves my father. He understands Dad's pride in his own strength, his work ethic and his strong conviction of what's right and wrong. Dad is the only father Ralphs ever had, that's why it hurts him so badly to see his strength slowly leave. He knows how humiliating it must feel. I think in a way it frightens Ralph and later on, when Dad is hospitalized, it explains why he refuses to see him.

Unlike dad, Ralph is very pragmatic, agnostic. One conversation that sent him into an emotional tailspin happened when Dad was still living in his apartment at Ron and Dixie's. During one of our Wednesday lunches the four of us were pondering the afterlife and whether ghosts existed. Dad listened, and then he casually said "I saw a ghost the other night. She was a young woman, dressed in old fashioned clothes and she came and stood in the doorway and just starred at me." I asked if it was Mom and he said no, that he had never seen her before. Poor Ralph was literally shaken to his core. On the way home he told me that he didn't believe in such mumbo-jumbo, but this was Dad telling us what he had seen. It bothered him for days, that quite possibly his views could be wrong, because if Stew said it happened, it happened.

Dear Diary:

I've always told Ralph that my dad would live to be a hundred, I just felt it. He'd give me a 'poor Mary' look, but today it appears that I might just be right after all. Sure, he's getting a little forgetful, but he comes right back to the present and knows exactly what's going on. This morning we talk non-stop even though Dad is slurring his words and his voice is getting weaker. When he is trying to recall something his brow will furrow and I can see the struggle, the physical struggle of him trying to remember and I feel like shouting, "Let it go, don't torture yourself, don't use up your remaining strength trying to remember some mundane thing like who was in yesterday!" His skin is yellow and he has a black eye, the result of a pimple he's picked, (he is always picking, usually at his scabby arms). I tell him that Ron and Dixie have a cow waiting to calf, but it just doesn't seem to want to come. He says that he'll get over and have a look at her. That is his one little slip. Does he really believe it can still happen?

He tells us Bob is coming weekend after next to take him for a drive. Bob later verifies this to be true. He laughs about getting out of bed the other night, and the nurse catching him at the door and asking where he was going. He told her he was going home and she reminded him that he was home. I ask him where he was really going and he says in all seriousness "'I don't know." He tells us that the reason he gets mixed up is because his dreams are so vivid. Kim comes in, lovely Kim, and we have a laugh about her dogs and horses and Rick—Red Light Rick, named for his ability to hit every red light in a fifty mile radius. Dad laughs easily.

When we got home and opened the garage door there was a young starling flopping around on the floor. It was still alive, but lying in a pool of grey guck, probably brain fluid from constantly banging against the window. Its eye was gone and I was surprised that its beak didn't seem to be broken. I picked it up and tried to warm it in my hands, noticing the colors of its wings, then took it out to put it under a tree. It had dug one claw into my finger so tightly that I could not pry it off and for a moment thought it had died. Finally I loosened its grip and lay it on the grass where it continued to struggle. I left it there and checked out the window a few minutes later and it was still throwing itself around in agony.

I couldn't let it die on the grass with the cold wind blowing, out in the open, unprotected, so I got a flower pot, lined it with paper towels, lay the bird in and loosely covered the top with a paper towel. I put it on the veranda and went into the house. I didn't know if it was dead or alive or even gone and I felt too vulnerable to go and look. The next day the flower pot was gone and I asked Ralph if it was dead and he said yes, dead and buried. Being as superstitious as I am, the bird incident affected me deeply, made me feel as if it was a glimpse into the future, what was to come.

Dear Diary:

Phil and his little Renee come today, our youngest grand-daughter. Our beautiful Renee with the pure heart wanted to see her G.G, but was reluctant. She called me the night before and seemed to be 'beating around the bush'. She was making small talk, but I knew something important was on her mind. Finally she just came right out and asked if I thought he would remember her. I assured her that he would, thinking "Please God" as I did so. When we walked in Dad looked sleepily at her. I asked if he knew who it was and he said, "Of course, it's Renee." It was a quiet visit, and when we left Renee was telling us that he hadn't changed at all, that he was the same G.G. as always.

Dear Diary:

Ron and Dixie appear today and what a pleasant surprise it is to see them. It has been weeks, maybe months since we've seen each other and we have so much catching up to do. It is a treat to talk about something else besides Dad's condition. We try not to 'talk over' him but of course we do. There is just so much news; hockey, travel, people we know. Dad listens to our conversation content and at ease. He perks up when we start talking about Ron and Dixie's two barn cats. He had told me that one got killed, stepped on by a cow. Today Dixie tells him he must have been thinking about some other cats because their two are still alive. He thinks for a while and says it must've been a dream and is very relieved to learn that the two cats that once gave him such pleasure are still around (not for long, such is the fate of the barn cat). Dad thinking the cat had been stepped on by a cow probably goes back to our childhood when we had a rabbit named 'Bunny Whitetail". We loved B.W and when I was in grade one Ron used to walk over to the school with the rabbit at recess and noon for the kids to see. Bunny used to drink milk from a bowl with the cats. One day a rambunctious calf stepped on the rabbit and killed him.

Dad's parents always had a house cat and I think that he would have liked one when we were growing up but Mom would never allow any animal in the house, even on the coldest of winter nights Laddie stayed in the garage. The closest we ever came to having a house cat was Daisy, a one eyed, black and white barn cat that hung around the house. We all really liked Daisy, even Dad, but one day Mom ran over her and we never had another take her place. We all wondered if Mom could've been a little more careful backing out of the garage. She was probably backing out to make the short drive to the end of the lane to get the mail.

My mother was not an animal lover, or even liker. She entered the barn only once, on a day in November, to tell dad that President Kennedy had been assassinated. Just to show how innocent those days were, my dad's reply was, "What does assassinated mean?"

Ron and Dixie went in yesterday morning and the secretary at the door said there was no use going up to his room because he wasn't there. They asked where he was and she said "Gone fishing". And so he had. Dad wasn't too impressed with the fishing trip. He only caught one and he was cold most of the day. When he came back he played bingo, had supper, and then watched the hockey game until 11 p.m.

That song 'Maybe I'm Amazed." keeps running through my head.

Dear Diary:

Right away he tells us that when he woke this morning he felt weak, just not right. Ralph laughs and says it's exhaustion from pulling in that huge fish. I find out that he is on antibiotics again and wonder why. He has a temperature and I help him change his wet shirt before lunch. He has also a deep phlegmy cough and diarrhea. We have a chuckle when he tells us that Dr. Phil was there last night. I tell him he should have asked Dr. Phil some questions while he had the chance.

As I suspect, he is sick. In my mind, the hell of the next six months began with that fishing trip. They took him by ambulance to the hospital when he began having difficulty breathing and constant, horrible diarrhea. I had never heard of C-Diff then and between the hospital blaming the nursing home and the nursing home blaming the hospital, I couldn't get any answers. When I looked it up on the computer I was horrified. It will take away every single scrap of esteem a person has ever had. My Dad is very ill, and it is time I should be thinking about funeral arrangements; instead I fiddle with pictures, clean the house, and go for long walks with Ruby, our sweet little, neurotic dog. I am afraid.

With no regard for his feelings, I insist that Ralph take me to the hospital every other day. He drops me off and he and Ruby go the park at Fairy Lake, the area where Ralph spent his childhood. They have nice peaceful walks. Not so great for me. Dad is in complete isolation which means that I have to cover up every inch of exposed skin to protect myself when I enter his room. I even have to wear an eye visor.

Dear Diary:

He is sleeping, but restless, his fingers going to his lips as if he is trying to put something in his mouth. I notice that he hasn't eaten his breakfast. When I touch him he wakes immediately, stares at me, and for a second, I don't think he knows who I am. He does. We try to talk, but his voice is almost non-existent. It is very frustrating because I feel he is saying important stuff, and I cannot hear him. I can't ask him to repeat what he's said because it takes too much of his strength. I do manage to understand the chilling words "I hope that this is it, the end. It doesn't matter if I get better, I'll just get sick again." He says he isn't afraid and is ready to go. I am about to say, "But Dad, I'm not ready for you to go", then catch myself and tell him I am so grateful to have had him for a father. All that stuff that he needs to hear but that I'm not ready to say. He says he has bad dreams, probably the meds, and when I ask him if he ever dreams about Mom he says, "She's here to help me." I can't bear not to touch him so remove my gloves and eventually my visor. I'll worry about it later. And worry I do when I get sick.

He dozes off and I rest my head on the germ covered bed railing, I remember when Dad and Mom bought their tomb stone. It was like a comedy skit. We kids just rolled our eyes. It seemed never-ending.

For months they debated and argued about what would be inscribed on the stone. Dad wanted a picture of a Belgium and the symbol of the United Church of Canada. Mom wanted something more artsy like a field of wheat or a beautiful sunset. She was constantly scanning photos and magazines. Dad only pretended to negotiate. He had made up his mind. Mom was really ticked off and would tell him often that you just did not put a likeness of a horse on a tombstone and it just proved how daft he really was, and now the whole world would see what she'd had to live with all these years. Maybe it was Betty, the horse that winked at him that holds the place of honor. Oh, and the stone has the names of us three kids, just so we will have to behave ourselves to avoid any embarrassment to Mom and Dad, for the rest of eternity.

Finally the stone was all done and in place, just waiting for the dates to be inscribed. One evening at dusk, they stood quietly at the site. Mom wondered out loud who would be the one standing alone in this same place. He said, "I hope you go first so that I can look after you, then I'll follow a few days later." He kind of recanted on that during one of our talks and said that he wished he'd gone first. It was just too painful to lose her. I assured him that it was as it should be. Mom was not strong enough to shoulder the loneliness.

I reluctantly pull myself back to the present and leave to talk to the nurses. On my way back I peek in at Dad. His eyes are closed and he is carrying on quite an animated conversation. I tap on the glass and he turns his head, opens one eye and doesn't acknowledge me, just goes back to talking. When I go out to the car Ralph asks how he is and I say he is dying.

Dixie phoned later that night and said Dad was just a little confused and that they had the best talk ever about farming. What the hell? This annoyed me, it could not be true, but then I thought, of course they could talk about farming. Dad didn't need to be aware to talk about farming, and Dixie was always the one he had the best conversations with. She knew most of the people he knew, referred to directions the way he did, "Go South, and then just before the Burns farm turn East till you come to the bridge and turn North." It was beyond me. Left and right, that's what I understood. The next day I called the hospital and spoke to his nurse. She said he was a joy, 'pleasantly confused.' She also said that he was coherent and talking about the farm. I wondered what farm.

Am I missing something, or seeing more? Am I the one in denial? Maybe he's not even as sick as I think he is. I don't want to do it anymore. Can't someone else do it, take the worry, the fear? Just let me have peace for a week or so. Take me to the safe place where he sometimes goes. Take me back to my childhood, cuddled on his lap, his strong arms holding me, laughing together. How long before our laughter stops forever?

Dear Diary:

The good news is that he is off the oxygen, but the bad news is that he still has C-Diff. and remains very contagious. He has thrush in the mouth and stone cold arms, yet complains of being hot and has a fan blowing on him constantly. I worry that if it gets too cold or annoying he can't reach it to shut if off or point it in another direction. At this point would he even know how? He just lies there and waits for someone to come in. A specialist came in to do a swallowing test and said that some of what he is eating and drinking is going down the wrong hole, into the lungs. Now I have a little extra to worry about, that he will choke to death, just like Mom. Ron went to visit him after we left and dad asked "Is there any possible way you can pull the plug on me? I've had enough and am ready to go." Ron gently told him there was no plug to pull.

Dear Diary:

He is sleeping, so soundly that I imagine it will be like this when he dies. They have him heavily drugged and he just can't keep his eyes open. He has a catheter in, full of bloody urine and is on oxygen again. I sit beside the bed and hold his hand, stroking his beautiful, soft hair. God how I love his hair, get such pleasure from the feel of it. Then I start to pray, with the tears getting in the way as always. "Dear God, please let him just stop breathing, let it be over, no more suffering or indignities. Please take him now, while I'm here." I am in such a disturbed state that I almost add, "I'll be a good girl, I will do anything you ask, just take away his suffering." I need to hold him, skin on skin, so am careless about my isolation garb again.

Dear Diary:

Today is our third trip to Aurora this week. Tired, but can't stay away. Ralph needs a rest from the traffic and the long drive, but I am selfish in my demands to go and my hysterics and tears wear him down. I care about nothing, think about nothing, but my father's struggle right now.

He looks better but is still in isolation, and very lonely and depressed. He doesn't understand why he can't just die. The diarrhea is not letting up and he is on a new (third) antibiotic that gives him bad dreams when he does manage to fall asleep. I think that it is the diarrhea that has taken away his will to live, the humiliation for such a proud man. His lip sores are worse and there are more of them. I tell him to stop touching them. I also tell him that it doesn't look as if now is his time and that he has to stop lying there just thinking. I have a television hooked up but he insists that he doesn't want one and won't watch it. I think he just doesn't want me to pay for it. He is still refusing all hospital food. Can he survive once again? Gut isn't giving him any nutrients and he is getting weaker and weaker. He is losing weight at an alarming rate. I decide that I have to talk to his nurse, to anyone who will give me some answers. When he's awake like today and I'm taking charge, he looks at me with his huge blue eyes, full of hope, as if I will give him just a shred of good news. I don't lie to him about his illness. I'm no saint, I would if I could. Maybe that's what he wants from me . . . . lies.

The talk with the nurse takes me down to a very dark place. I didn't think I could fall any further. She tells me the C-diff will last another two months, and when it does go away will come back. C-diff is a virus that attacks the good bacteria in the bowel. Most people don't know how dangerous it is or how common.

It is literally a killer in nursing homes and hospitals. An added worry is that his room at the nursing home will be held for only twenty one days. Will they take him back if he shows positive for C-diff?

Ron and Dixie visit the next day, and he tells them about all the neat stuff he is watching on television. My hair is turning as white as his.

I know that many others go through this and feel the same pain and confusion that I'm feeling. I wonder if they too question a God that gives such a full, rich, proud life only to let the break-down of the body return a man to the state of a child. I think of my Mother's saying "Once a man, twice a child." Not for one moment did I ever think it would describe my Dad. No control, that's the kicker, that's what sucks. There's little I can do but watch and pray that it will soon be over, but also pray that he will improve, for just a little while longer. Karen called last night to tell me that he has started to eat. He wants to go back to the nursing home.

Dear Diary:

He's back at the home, and on a very strong anti-biotic to try to get rid of the C-diff which keeps coming back. He's trying hard to eat, to try to gain back some weight, but his strength is gone, he has no appetite and fears diarrhea when he does eat.

Today he looks like what he is, a very sick man. Sheet half on, catheter tube full of bloody urine, yellow skin. However his mind is as sharp as a teenagers, actually not a great comparison, teenagers are not usually a beacon of brightness. I can understand why Socrates stated "Youth is wasted on the young.' I digress.

He is very funny, witty. "You know Ralph, you should quit smoking, If you don't you'll be in this bed when I'm done with it." Then he asks me if I remember the time Mom threw a cigarette out the car window and it blew back in, setting the car on fire. We had an attached garage at the time so she almost burned the house down.

We talk about Moms save the children from smoking plan. When we were young Mom used to smoke Cameo cigarettes and always kept them hidden in her bedroom drawer. It would be a terrible thing if a neighbor or, heaven forbid, the Minister dropped in and saw a package of cigarettes in the house.

Knowing where the cigarettes were kept meant easy pickings for us kids, and every time she would realize that one of her stash was missing she never said a word, but put a little note in the package about how disappointed she was in us and just put the cigarettes back in the drawer. She would also include magazine and newspaper clippings about the dangers of smoking. Unfortunately it didn't work very well. Dad enjoys this conversation and when he smiles, it takes away all of the signs of illness, as if none of this is happening. I store the mind-picture deep down, where I can get it when I need it.

We laugh, and talk and remember. We recall the fall days when the wheat would be harvested. Dad was always popping wheat into his mouth and chewing it, then spitting it out. I don't know whether it was his way of testing for quality or if he just liked the taste. He reminds us about the time Ron and I ran away to avoid going to the dentist. After all these years he remembers. "The dentist was old Dr. Snider. Your Mother was so mad because he said that if you were his kids you wouldn't be able to sit down for a week."

It all started with the much feared dentist appointment. Dad had another farm at Victoria Square at this time and made daily trips. This day he was hauling wheat with the truck. Ron and I decided to bury ourselves in the wheat, go to Victoria Square, and miss the dentist appointment. When we finally popped up and tapped on the back window of the truck it was too late to turn back. Mom had to call the dentist and say truthfully "I've looked everywhere and can't find them". These stories are like medicine to Dad and they make him feel a heck of a lot better than the real stuff ever can.

I talk to Ron and Dixie or Bob and Karen almost every day. We all have different theories on how long he'll be able to continue to go on with all the ups and downs. I think he will die soon, Ron doesn't want to talk about his death, but says that "Dad can only go to the well so many times," and Bob feels we should get on with our lives and just wait and see. They all think I'm too caught up in what-ifs, what might happen.

Bob is older and wiser. He probably learned the lessons I am struggling with years ago. He just goes with the flow, has quiet talks with Dad. He is like a ghost. He slips in and out without anyone knowing about it. He tells me that he asked Dad if he had any regrets about his life, and dad said just one. Bob was truly expecting him to say he wished he hadn't of worked so hard, had spent more time with his family or not been so hard on Bob when he was a boy, instead Dad's reply was "I wish I had've been a vet." It was news to all of us, he'd never mentioned it.

The three of us decide to tell the nursing home that unless he falls and breaks a hip, or can't breathe we don't want him to go back to the hospital. We want him where he feels safe.

My Dad is to me a genuine Christian. He walks the walk, yet not once as a child did I hear him mention one word of religion to us kids. That was Mom's job. He simply showed us through example how we should live. He never missed church and Mom told me once that it was annoying when she felt tired or not well on a Sunday morning and he would start to pull out his suit. If she said she didn't feel like going his answer was always the same, "Fine, stay home." She would feel guilt and drag herself from her bed to start planning what stunning outfit she would wear that day.

Even though it seemed very personal, I wondered about Dad's relationship with God now near the end of his life. One day, during one of our quiet talks I asked him if he ever thought about God. He said, "Nope, don't need to." I found his reply rather startling but I fully understood. He didn't need any last minute reprieves. At least that's the way I saw it, on that particular day. These talks that I have with my Father leave me worn out. It's such new territory I don't know how to live in it, like a refugee in a foreign country.

A true example of my Dad's kindness to others involved a homeless man who rode his bike summer and winter. He carried a broom and had a compulsion to sweep the highway along Wellington Street. He would stride to the middle of the road, hold up his hand to stop traffic and begin to sweep, seemingly unfazed by the honking of car horns and angry words. He intrigued the heck out of all of us. He had a job to do and would not stop until it was done, then he would climb back on his bike and head for the next area that needed cleaning. The thing that made all of us so very curious was that when he wasn't busy sweeping streets he would sit under a tree and write. He was constantly writing in an old, gnarled notebook. What was he writing? Was it pure nonsense or a detailed journal of his life? Was he a fool or a genius?

When there was an event at the church during the winter, he'd quietly go upstairs where there were no people and sit in the last pew to soak up a little warmth. Aside from the Sunday service, a lot of the social functions were held in the basement of the church, where the kitchen was. This particular evening was the annual church supper. Dad had seen him go upstairs earlier and at one point filled a plate and took it up to him. When I heard this several days later I was full of questions. "What did he say? What was he writing? "Thank you was all he said." Dad replied, "And he wasn't writing anything, the pages were blank."

Dad also mentioned to the man that there was a good warm coat that someone had left about a year ago and offered it to him. "Don't need it," the man said, "Already got one." I think they could've been good friends if they'd met earlier and under different circumstances. Both said and took only what was needed.

The nurses tell us that Dads doing better. He's up in his wheelchair but doesn't want to leave his room. Not only has this disease invaded his body but his ego too. The C-Diff has left him fifty pounds lighter, maybe more. He isn't much over a hundred pounds and his legs won't hold even this minimal weight. No wonder he wants to stay in his room. Dad always felt pride and would declare often (very often) that he has weighed the same his entire adult life—154 pounds. The weight loss has to be just another, I guess you could say, loss.

Dear Diary:

Almost as soon as we arrive he drifts off to sleep and I sit and stroke his arms. I feel a strong yearning to hold him like a child, tell him everything will be alright. I also feel a need to be back to a time when I was curled up on his knee, in his big chair. My Mother was telling him to send me off to bed, but I wanted to stay up to watch I Love Lucy. He said it wasn't on and I said it was; it says so right here in the paper. He said "No, that say's I Love Louie." Isn't it ironic, this is a reversal of all that we were?

He asks me to read the latest card or note from Karen, even the old ones that he has saved. When Bob and Karen are in Florida or away on the Harley she sends him a lot of mail, just to let him know that he is in their thoughts. No matter where they are she calls me every Wednesday night to see how he was that day.

It is slightly frightening to enter a nursing home for the first time. There are smells that unsettle you right away. Often the odor of food cooking can be enough to make you feel nauseated, and there is always the faint scent of urine. Nurses are rushing around, cheerfully trying to calm a screaming resident or encourage another into a tub. But it's the people themselves that leave you feeling unprepared and anxious to flee. They sleep in their wheelchairs, wherever they have been set in the morning, heads hanging down, as if there is no bone structure in their necks. Yet if you speak out loud they come back to life, hoping that even though they don't recognize you that you might be there to see them. Then there are the few who seem to be living in some sort of hell. They cry out for Mothers and Fathers gone long ago, and children and other loved ones who have stopped coming because, really, what's the sense, there is no recognition, on either side. These people seem as if their souls are lost, searching, struggling for peace. Where are they?

Dear Diary:

Dad is upset when we arrive because he says that they weighed him and he only weighs thirty-five pounds. I explain that it is in kilos and lie to convince him that it is a good weight in pounds. He's drinking and eating a bit, but when I put my hand on his leg I am amazed at how small it is. The weight loss and inability to stand seem to bother him more than anything. He is sad and in pain. "I feel sorry for anyone that lives over ninety, I wouldn't wish that on any person." he grumbles. I'm just about to tell him about the many vibrant people who are over ninety and living productive lives, but realize how cruel that would be. Besides, I don't know that many. His skin is a definite yellow color. I check the whites of his eyes, and they look fine, still I wonder if the cancer has invaded his liver.

I ask how he is feeling, really feeling and he says it's always the same. I gently persist and finally he says it's the pain in his back when he sits or even lies down. It never goes away. He knows that the cancer is in his bones. I ask about upping pain medication and he agrees and when I speak to the nurse she says that he can have all the pain medication he needs and that he should ask before the pain becomes intolerable. That's where the problem lies, that's the kicker. He won't ask, sees it as weakness, and doesn't want to bother the nurses. He waits until they see his distress, or until I come and the first thing he does is send me running to get him pain medication.

I tell him that I have cancelled my trip to Spain and he says 'good' which is totally out of character for him. Usually he will say, "Go, I'll be fine," then he will add with a slight grin in Ralph's direction, "You know, one of these days they'll be bringing her home in a box, right Ralph?" Ralph's agreement makes such a dark subject become comical. We kids are all travelers and we sure didn't get it from him. Dad hated travel. This was tough on Mom who wanted to be on the move constantly. Part of the problem was that he couldn't leave the farm, and the other part was that he wanted his own bed, his own food, his own home and above all, he just didn't want to go. Mom once talked him into taking a cruise to Mexico. They were going to an evening performance of a play and at the last minute Mom had to go to the bathroom. When they entered the theatre it was pitch black and they couldn't find their seats. As they were floundering in the dark, dad fell into the orchestra pit. The performance was stopped, the lights went up and the announcer asked if there was a doctor in the house. Dad was unhurt, totally humiliated, and complained for years that he lost his good jack knife in that pit, the knife he used to cut the string on the hay bales.

When Mom would tell this story she would be laughing so hard she would have difficulty getting the words out. My Mom's laughter was almost holy to me. I seldom laughed myself. Her laughter was loud and hearty and when she pulled me in with her it took away my breath and caused tears to run down my cheeks.

The boys didn't always appreciate her humor.

Dad didn't make us laugh in the same way. We laughed *at* him when he would get caught at something, because he was so seemingly perfect. Things like the Income Tax people heading up the driveway brief cases in hand, or when he bought a three teated cow from a neighbor. He grumbled about that one for a very long time. Mom always said that it would be funny if during a Bingo game someone called Bingo and didn't have the numbers. It happened to Dad on that same cruise to Mexico. God she must have had a good time. He went to Japan under real duress and ended up coming home alone, all that way. He said all there was to eat was fish, you had to sleep on the floor and there were too many foreigners.

Now the nurse says that if the catheter doesn't come out he will have a U.I. infection, and more antibiotics and probably another dose of C-Diff. I feel like screaming "Well take it the hell out then!" Another nurse says his skin will soon begin to break down if he doesn't move more, get out of bed. The doctor gave him an examination and had the nurse call the family to see if we wanted a feeding tube inserted or to send him to the hospital. Of course not, on both counts. The doctor also wanted to know how the family wanted to proceed. Why are they even asking? They know how we feel. We are saying do nothing. He is fairly comfortable, drinking well and eating a bit. No extra measures are necessary unless he is in distress. Hospitalization is to be a last resort. I called down on Saturday and Liza said that he had a really good day. He'd gotten up for all three meals, wheeled himself down to the dining room. She said everyone was glad to see him and he had a big smile on his face.

Dear Diary:

This week he is just lying there wide awake, waiting. I can't get over how someone can lose fifty pounds and their head still remain the same—no hollow cheeks, eyes brilliant blue. As time goes on the color of his eyes seem to become more vivid. With his body covered by sheets he doesn't look as if he's lost any weight at all. He says that he feels sick when he eats and the other night at supper vomited in front of everyone. What can I say, what can I do? I feel so broken, so hurt. There's nothing to do, nothing to say, only misery. Now, he is quiet, still tormented by the humiliation in the dining room.

I get him some pain medication and when the nurse brings it in I start to tell her about the time he took one of Mom's sleeping pills. He perks right up and I can see his mind preparing excuses before I even began the story.

Mom was experiencing some chest pain late one afternoon and Dad decided that she should go to the emergency department. After waiting for hours, the hospital said they were going to keep her all night, just to be on the safe side. Dad was tired from the long day and when he got home he decided, for the first time ever, to take one of Mom's sleeping pills. Adult kids often question the decisions of aging parents and many, many times over the years I've had to force myself to just keep quiet, let it go. But when I heard about this episode I wondered, why would he do that? What was he thinking? What if Mom went bad in the night and he was needed? She didn't go bad, just the opposite, she went good, and the hospital called at midnight for him to come and get her. He made it to the hospital, got her loaded into the car, and didn't fall asleep until he started to make the turn from Bayview onto Wellington Street. The car rolled on its side and they barely missed a hydro pole. A police officer drove them home, Mom complaining that she would've stayed in the hospital if she had known he was going to try to kill her. "I didn't fall asleep, just missed the turn in the dark" Dad says when I finish the story and it leads to good humored teasing.

Dad missed a few turns. He and Mom's house had a parking area off to one side of the house. It was to back into to turn around after backing out of the garage. He had an old truck that he had bought from the Hydro when they were done with it. After a good ten years of use it became a horrible, unsafe truck that shouldn't have been on the road. Whenever one of the family drove it they were horrified that such an unsafe vehicle was dad's daily means of transportation. The brakes were almost non-existent, the transmission made noises as if it could drop out at any time and it shook so bad that papers and mail sitting on the dashboard would flutter to the floor. The glove box would open if he hit speeds over 50kms an hour which was seldom. But you never, ever said anything negative about that truck. He loved it and thought that it drove as well as a new truck.

Ralph and I got a new truck of our own and we drove down one Sunday to show Mom and Dad. Dad went out to do the chores and forgot about our truck being parked in the turn-around and backed into it. The second time it happened we had a car and the last time Karen watched helplessly from the kitchen window as he plowed into their car. When these things happened it just reinforced how stubborn, he could be. You never submitted the damage to the insurance company. They would 'take you to the cleaners'. Dad always knew a small garage, run by a good man, an honest man, and there our vehicles went, and often sat for weeks waiting for parts.

Around this time period I was working for the Board of Education in Aurora. One day I got called into my boss's office. He was so serious that I felt as if I'd done something terribly wrong. "Mary" he began, "You have to do something about your Father. He pulled out of the driveway this morning and proceeded to putter up the road in that old white truck. It was bumper to bumper traffic and cars were lined all the way up the hill. No one could get past him. You had better speak to him before he causes an accident." I said I would, but I didn't. What was the use?

Dear Diary:

I don't kiss him goodbye anymore for fear of getting sick again, but when I hug him as hard as I dare and my face sinks into his pillow I think, "Might as well kiss him, his pillow probably has more germs than his face." For no reason at all I mention a time, about sixty years ago, when I carried around a baby chick in a tea cup. The chick was dead. When I picked it up and its little neck flopped to one side I remember saying, "Daddy, I think it's dead." "Yup" he replied "Looks like it is." Did it really happen or is it just fragments of some long-forgotten dream? Is it possible to remember minute images like this for decades? My Father grinned, "It wasn't dead when I put it in the cup. Clayton was there that day."

Things aren't great at home. My son doesn't want to hear about Dad's distress every time we have a conversation, my daughter thinks I'm depressed (you think?), and my husband remains mute, not knowing how to help me. They don't understand my need to have Dad in my thoughts every moment of every day. All I know is that I like thinking about him, talking about him and remembering. I'll deal with the fallout at home after it's all over. Start to rebuild. I wonder what Bob and Karen are feeling or Ron and Dixie or even the grandchildren who can't even imagine a life without their Grandfather.

Maybe they are just waiting for the axe to fall, and then they'll think about it. Not me. I have to see the axe fall. Imagine how the end will be and when he's good I imagine a peaceful ending, with family all around, everyone saying their goodbyes, a room filled with love, flowers and hymns playing on a CD player. Then I stop long enough to remind myself what a fool I am.

Bob was in to see Dad the other night and Dad told him that he didn't want to live any longer, not many friends left, no wife, and no dignity. Bob felt he was telling him the end was near.

I cry easily. I cry when I'm feeling sad and even though I feel sad a lot of the time and cry buckets of tears, I know that I should be dancing in the streets that my Father has lived as long as he has, and so well. Dad used to cry at happy events. He was very sentimental about his family. He once had to make a speech at his and Mom's sixtieth wedding anniversary and couldn't do it. Dad's been making speeches his entire adult life, but this special night when he stood up to speak, his hand went to his pocket and he started to fiddle with his change. Bob always said that this was a bad sign. When Dad started fiddling with the change in his pocket tears were quick to follow. This night he had been attempting to say to Mom, "You are as beautiful today as the day I married you," but couldn't continue and just hugged her and sat down. Mom tried to smile, but it wasn't a real genuine smile. She had written the speech, and he goofed up right in the most important part! Another time the family was at a birthday celebration for Aunt Agnes. The smokers were outside, and the trunk of Dad's car kept going up all by itself. At first the group wondered what on earth was wrong with the car, and then Bob realized what was happening. The party inside must have turned emotional and Dad's fiddling with his change was hitting his keys and setting the trunk off. Bob went in and told him, but a few minutes later the trunk was going up again

Dear Diary

This Wednesday I am crying because I hurt him, I physically hurt him. I was getting him up for lunch and following my regular routine. I put his slippers on while he was still in bed, then gently put one arm behind his shoulders and the other under his knees to sit him up. When I tried to pivot him to the wheel chair his legs gave out and I could barely keep from dropping him. He cried out in pain. What a big mistake on my part, trying to do it alone. As we were waiting to leave and I was holding him, saying goodbye he appeared translucent. It was pain, and I had made it worse. He has tested positive for C-Diff again.

The drive home was one of those stare out the window drives when I just don't have the strength or inclination to engage in any sort of conversation with Ralph. I watch the terrain, and when I see a path beside the road (likely made by dirt bikes and snow mobiles) I pretend that I'm horseback riding along that path. If it goes uphill, I trot; if it's smooth I feel the joy of a good canter. I follow the path till it ends. The cold, blustery weather reminds me of my Dad plowing a field beside a church. It was when he owned the second farm at Victoria Square. I was very young, not in school yet, and it was bloody cold. I was on his knee on the tractor. We were trying to keep each other warm. There was a funeral going on at the church and we watched as they lowered the body into the ground. "Wish I was in there with him" Dad suddenly said. His dying had never occurred to me and I asked him if he was going to die, and he answered "Hadn't planned on it. I was just thinking about how warm it would be in that hole."

How can he change from week to week? One week I know he's dying and I get back to making arrangements and the next week he's better. He thinks about others even as he gets sicker and sicker. If he feels sick to his stomach or has to go to the bathroom he doesn't like to bother the girls so he will attempt to get from the bed to the wheelchair by rolling. What happens when he finally reaches the bathroom is beyond me. How can he manage?

Still funny things happen, little episodes that lighten my life just a little. I was in my favorite dress shop last week looking for a dress for the inevitable funeral. One of the girls said "You know Mary; you've been in here once each season looking for a dress for your Father's funeral." We all broke into morbid laughter, and I laughed the hardest. It's the same with the kids. It seems I'm always calling to tell them to get ready, to decide on clothes, speak to their bosses, make sure their cars are running well because their grandfather will be gone within the week. I wonder when they stopped listening. Like the little boy who called wolf, when the time comes they won't believe it.

Dear Diary:

Dad's ninety-fifth birthday is coming up and I ask if he wants a notice put in the paper. He says no, that people will just feel they have to come or send a card. My mind wanders and I start making plans for a celebration like we used to have at Vandorf Hall. He could come in his wheelchair and see all his old friends, and we could have sandwiches and a birthday cake. I snap back to the present, and the joy of what once was is replaced by all familiar sadness. I feel these two emotions in a ridiculously short time span. I ask him if he remembers the birthday dinners Mom used to make. She'd bake a cake and put out all the best silver and make a real big deal out of it. He'd get about fifty birthday cards, if not more. He remembers, "That damn dog of yours throwing up under the dining room table one time while we were eating." I laugh, slightly embarrassed and the only retort I can come up with is, "True, that was Spencer but remember when Ruby was a puppy and she pooped in Mom's shoe and Mom didn't realize it until she was half way out to the mailbox?"

It is sort of like a hockey game with the wins and losses. I've seen him lose badly then rally for an unexpected win. I now know what to expect. There might be a couple of last minute goals, and he might even win a game or two, but he won't make the play offs.

Dear Diary:

Today he is just lying there, not watching television or even sleeping. His eyes are dark and he looks so very tired. He tells us some impossible things, like he walked over to the farm yesterday. I go out into the hall to let go of the tears that are so close to over flowing that I am holding my breath. The nurses have grown accustomed to seeing me kneeling on the floor outside his room, weeping in misery and frustration. Some take me in their arms and others look at me as if to say 'I understand, cry if you need to'. They comfort me. The head nurse tells me that the doctor feels that Dad is confused and depressed and put him on Celexa, an anti-depressant. The actions of some of these 'healers' boggles my mind. By the time the drug kicks in he could be dead. An antidepressant? Of course he's freaking depressed. The nurse also says that dad is very difficult at night, trying to get out of bed to do the chores. She wants to know what I think about putting him in restraints. I tell her he'd go ballistic, and they had better stay clear. Then I think how foolish that must sound. He weighs less than a hundred pounds, stay clear of what, who? Not my Father, he left a long time ago.

Dear Diary:

Today is the second trip down this week and when we enter the room he is sleeping soundly. I try to wake him and honestly can't. I know he hasn't died because his skin is warm, but then I begin to think that he has slipped into a coma. I rub his arms, whisper in his ear, and stroke his face. Finally he wakes up, not even drowsy, just back from wherever he's been. He gives a little chuckle when I remind him that if there's a fall election he'd better vote for Harper. He has been going down for all meals again and still transferring himself from bed to wheelchair. He won at Bingo again last night. There used to be a horse on the jumping circuit called Stoic. That's how I think of my dad . . . stoic . . . and so he is. No complaining, just getting on with his life and the time he has left.

When Emily, Kelly's daughter was little she asked him what he was going to be when he grew up. He answered, 'An angel'. We smile at the memory and I realize that this is a good time to bring up questions about his funeral. The fact it has to be talked about at all, makes me uneasy and for some reason a little angry. I don't want to do it. What if he is feeling good, and thinking that he just may squeeze in another year, and I start talking about funeral arrangements? My hands are sweaty and I wipe them on my jeans. It's not an easy subject to just kind of ease into. We talk about the small things like the minister, location and flowers (he doesn't want any, just for people to use the money to help out a family in need). It is a short conversation, somber, and we are both relieved when his two favorite nurses rush in loud and giddy. One is telling us a story and laughing so hard she can hardly speak. Apparently yesterday, after giving Dad his shower, she made his hair into a Mohawk and then took him into the bathroom and they looked in the mirror and both laughed and laughed. Now he looks at me and with a smile on his face says the whole thing was entirely my fault because he was out of Brylcreem again!

Brycreem, a little dab'll do ya. He's used it since I was a child, never used anything else on his hair, except for the time that Mom thought he was looking a little old and talked him into trying one of those comb in hair colors. His hair turned an ugly, dark shade that really was the color of what he shoveled out of the barn every day.

What he shoveled out of the barn every day once saved his life. A freezing day in January he fell out of the top story of the barn landing on his head. If he hadn't have just shoveled out a pile of warm, steaming manure he would have broken his neck. He landed smack in the middle of it. Like a giant dart board.

Dad once had an accident that had the potential to be more serious than any of the others, yet it's one that always makes me laugh. After Mom died Dad was out in front of the house working on the ride lawn mower. He tripped, went down hard and couldn't get back up. Poor innocent Brad, Ron and Dixie's son, was driving by in his cement truck and thought 'Oh, there's grandpa working on the lawn mower'. Brad had driven past the driveway, but decided to turn around and stop in to say a quick hello. Dad insisted that Brad help him stand up, but they just couldn't get him on his feet. Brad wanted to call 911 but Dad had a better idea. Brad would back the huge cement truck up until the passenger's door was right beside Dad, then the two of them could hoist him up into the truck and Brad could take him to the hospital. Can't see how that wouldn't work. So Brad started backing up, windows down listening to Dad's instructions. He couldn't see Dad who was lying on the ground, and the chances of running over him were very real. They finally positioned the truck, but of course Dad couldn't get in. Long story short, he had a broken hip and an ambulance had to be called. Brad was traumatized for days. What if he had been the one to run over grandpa? I like to joke with Dad about this one and to hear him give every excuse in the book for their inability to get him in the truck, everything but a broken hip.

Dear Diary:

His color is good and he appears to be in no apparent pain His blue eyes are sparkling and even his voice is strong. Last week Ralph had told me to prepare for his death, within the next couple of weeks, today he looks invigorated. When we visit Dad we often end up talking about some four-legged creature. Today it is our childhood dog Laddie, and how much Mom and Dad trusted him to take care of us and protect us.

He was a collie-shepherd mix, and he didn't have a tail, just a stub. Ron and I found out that there was going to be a dog show at the Aurora Horse Show and one of the categories was 'dog with the shortest tail'. It was a shoe-in, a given. Of course we'd win. Laddie's tail was so short it was non-existent. We were so excited. We'd win a cash prize and a ribbon. We brushed him and tried to find a suitable rope. Unfortunately, the only rope we could find was a big one, a barn rope, used for what purpose I have no idea. It was huge, as thick as our arms and very, very long. The day finally arrived and Laddie, unfixed and a fighter went after everything that moved—dogs, horses, and old women. Ron and I could barely hold him. He was a big dog, and we were being dragged around at the end of a six foot rope. Mom told us later that she and Dad decided that, under the circumstances, it would be a good idea to pretend they didn't know us, so they just watched from the side lines. It was horrible, and even at that young age we felt the humiliation of being starred at and worse, laughed at. Finally, the judging began and revenge would be ours. When they announced our category we somehow got Laddie close to the judge who was smugly holding his little ruler. He cautiously, very cautiously, stroked the dog's head, and then proceeded to the other end. When he lifted up his stub he declared him ineligible, because he didn't have a tail to measure. Somehow I think it was more than that. By now their humor had changed to pity and Mom and Dad got us out of there as quickly as they could. As soon as we were out of town Dad opened the car door and told Laddie to get out. He made it home shortly after us, having stopped only long enough to catch us a gift, a big groundhog. As soon as we had all settled down and were sitting on the porch, complaining about how we'd been cheated, our wonderful dog showed his appreciation for the day by disemboweling our gift all over the lawn.

CHAPTER V

The Crops Are Wilting

Karen called this week to say that Patrick, her grandson, a paramedic, was in to see his grandfather and that he seemed to have a gurgle in his chest. I called Dixie and she said that he did have a cough and was phlegmy. We talked about our promise to him that he would die at the home.

It's Thanksgiving, and I yesterday I wrote a letter that I wanted to read at my Father's funeral. The words flowed easily and I enjoyed doing it. Words come effortlessly when I write, but when I speak or read out loud they get all tangled up. When I told Phil what I was writing he said in his gentle way that I would not be able to do it, to get up and speak (read) at the funeral. He was right, of course. I deleted the letter, but what pleasure I got from writing it and thanking my Dad, and saying goodbye. I know I should have saved it and packed it away, but I didn't. It somehow was enough just to write it.

Dear Diary:

I feel pretty today. Nice jacket, jeans, hair good, even a little makeup. As we drive I smile with pleasure, remembering when Kelly and I took Alana to the fair last year. I was feeling good that day too and I noticed one of those age and weight guessers and I felt so good I thought I'd give it a try. She guessed me to be eight years younger and was way off on my weight. I won two stuffed animals for Alana. I was just so puffed up, eight years younger! I could hardly wait to tell Dad and when I did he said, "She couldn't have been very good could she?" It took me right down to earth where I belonged and the ironic thing about the whole conversation is that he was right! She must have been new on the job. Maybe the fair people said to her, "You don't have to run the merry-go-round today, try your hand at age guessing."

Driving down this morning the leaves in the distance are so strikingly beautiful that if the scene could be caught on canvas the only criticism would be that it doesn't look very realistic, the colors are too vivid.

It's not a great visit. He is drifting away and staying there longer, but it's his eyes that haunt me today. They are confused and darting around the room as if he isn't comfortable in his skin, as if he's afraid, something that I've never seen before. I attempt to keep him in the present, with me, but no matter how hard I try, I just can't do it.

Driving home I feel brittle, even my teeth hurt. I feel ugly and wrinkled and used. It is an effort to speak, I just want to look out the window and think. Think? There's nothing to think about, only speculation where my mind spends most of its days. I'm so tired, so tired of it all, but I can't rest until he is at peace. Even my dreams are filled with thoughts of my Father. It seems that I spend my days like a three year old just learning about the world, asking 'why' a dozen times an hour. There's so much. What will happen to him when he dies? Where will he go? Will he go anywhere? Will all the good things he did on earth just be one more memory for us, is that his reward? Will he suffer?

Dear Diary:

He is slurring his words, obviously heavily medicated, and coughing up a lot of mucus. He keeps drifting off to sleep in the middle of a conversation, and then he'll catch himself and insist that we stay. He tells us that Dixie brought in a picture of every single calf born this year, just for him to see. He could pour over each one and predict its future. One of those simple acts of kindness that mean so much. We were talking about his dreams, which we like to do, and I asked him if he dreamt about Mom and he thought for a minute and said he had a dream where he was on one side of a river, and Mom and all his relatives and friends were on the other side laughing and waving. I asked him what he thought it meant and he said, "I think it was Heaven". As we were leaving he said, 'I think I'll just go to sleep one of these days and not wake up." On the way home I felt a little sick to my stomach. I wondered what would happen to the family after he was gone. Would they divide? Would our strong heritage be finished? He is, after all, the glue that holds us together. It would be bad enough losing him, but to lose all the others, have them just drift away, would break my already fractured heart.

Dear Diary:

Kelly and her girls, Alana and Emily came with us today. I wasn't sure how Alana would react seeing Dad in his present condition but she was fine, great in fact. What an amazing child/woman. She gently kissed his forehead upon arrival and leaving, and at one point she said, clear as a bell "How are you feeling?" Alana is mentally challenged. Even though he was feeling very down, he couldn't help laughing at Emily when she stuck her studded tongue out at him. "You'll get tetanus with that thing in your mouth and end up losing your tongue." He's the same, maybe a bit worse, thinner for sure, not real responsive. There was a new male R.N. and when he came in with noon meds and put the head of the bed up Dad turned deathly pale, I was kissing him goodbye at the time. Pain? Head rush? Actually the nurse was a bit of a prick when I tried talking to him. Should have told him to find a job he was good at. He did tell me that dad has pneumonia—still, again, permanently? It just never seems to go away.

The nursing home has H1 (swine flu). The nurses are all getting their shots, but the facility is terribly understaffed. I haven't seen Dad for almost two weeks. Liza told me on the phone that he would insist on Wednesdays that we were coming. It didn't matter how many times she explained that we couldn't until the flu cleared. I have been sick myself and don't know what to do. He is becoming more confused each day, and if family stops going because of the flu he'll go somewhere and won't come back. He won't remember that we are staying away until the danger passes.

Winston Churchill was plagued by depression his whole adult life. He used to call it the black dog and often made references about being followed around by the black dog. Today the black dog is nipping at my heels.

Dear Diary:

Finally we get to see him. He is very confused, but it's a good confusion, he's in a happy place with friends and family on the farm. He told us that he, his brother Charlie and other brother Norman were building a small outdoor building and they built themselves in, forgot to put in a door. It brought him so much pleasure and he laughed as he wondered how they could do such a thing. The 'leaving' is gradual. He will tell us that Robert was in, that Mark has moved into their new home, how little Kyle is doing playing hockey, details. Then he'll say how late he was getting back last night, how he and his fellow farmers worked all day. He talked about Mary sitting on the big horse while he did the chores. I asked if he meant Aunt Mary or me (not sure what era he was in) and he said you. Back and forth, here and there, up and down.

His mental and physical condition are rapidly declining and the pain has set in big time. He asked me to go and get him some pain medication and the head nurse was concerned because he'd had two pills at nine and it was only eleven thirty, not even noon. She came down to his room and talked to him, evaluating his pain level. She asked him on a score of one to five what his level was and he said a four. Lord, that's a bad sign. She gave him a tablet and asked if one was enough and he said no and she gave him the second one. This shows me that the doctor's orders are to give him all the medication he needs, and that the pain is intolerable.

He has been complaining that his wheel chair digs in right at the bad part of his spine, and it led into a comical conversation about the wheel chair. I was on a tangent about Wal-Mart starting to sell caskets in the States. I have about a thousand things that make me mad in this world and Wal-Mart's one of them. He said that Walt told him that he could've gotten a wheelchair the same as the one he has now at Wal-Mart for a hundred and forty-nine dollars. Dad was mad because he paid eight hundred for his (true) and tongue-in-cheek I told him that it sounded as if he got cheated. He said yes and that his wheelchair wasn't even new. When I asked why he thought that, he said he measured it out with his fingers and one arm is 1\2 inch shorter than the other one. God, you gotta love this man. Suddenly he put his hand on his chest, as if in pain, and I asked, a bit panicky, "What's the matter with your chest?" And he grinned and said, "Boney".

When my heart is full, and especially when it's empty, I often whisper I love you, only to get his usual refrain, "Yup, yup." I feel his struggle to give back the appropriate words, especially now that he hasn't much time. Physically he cannot say the words. They will not leave his tongue. He has never been able to and it used to hurt Mom's feelings a bit. He doesn't trust the words, feels that love doesn't need to be confirmed verbally but by actions. So many times, he'd tell us he'd see a couple in public being overly affectionate only to go home to a nightmarish existence with each other. He did make a last ditch attempt to pacify Mom, when they were in their eighties, by buying her a valentine with the dreaded three words. We kids and the grandchildren got quite a kick out of this. "Dad bought mom a valentine!" I also distrust the words although I have no reason to, except I agree with my Dad.

You die as you live, this I know to be true. He's making sure everything's in place before he goes, tying up all the loose ends the way he always has. Today I hold on to him, not wanting to ever let go, finally I disengage myself, and we leave.

Dear Diary:

This week I notice a difference in the staff. They are still very good with him and with us, but everything's changed. The candy jar doesn't need much filling anymore. It's almost as if they are avoiding us. Not that they aren't friendly when we arrive and when I call, but I can see the pity in their eyes. There is no more hope, and they tell me without words that the end is nearer than I expect. They don't stop in to joke with him about running away together or how he had 'bed head' that morning. They don't pop in to ask us about our drive down, or the weather. They don't come in at all. Does he wake each morning to gentle hands that remember his pain, or has he gotten too heavy and a lot of work? Will today be the day he goes to the farm and doesn't come back? He told me Bob was sleeping in the big chair the night before, watching over him. Who knows?

My escapes from the room came often today, and each time I would make an excuse to get out of there Ralph would give me a look as if to say 'don't leave me here alone'. Ralph is hard of hearing and trying to have a conversation with Dad was impossible. He was so medicated that he couldn't stay awake. The nurses told me that the cancer is very aggressive on his right side. What would bring the tears was his struggle, real struggle to stay in the here and now, to stay awake, to keep up a conversation. That's what hurt. You know how it is when a baby is drifting off to sleep, how their little eyes flutter before they finally close, then just when you'd think they are asleep they give a little jerk and the eyes open again. That was my Father today. Even now, at the end of his days, he still tries to keep us there, fill us in on family news. Every time there would be a lull in the conversation he'd be asleep again, making chewing motions, mumbling, jumping as if something had startled him. He slurred his words so badly that I had to pretend to understand what he was saying. He was switching between family news to events that only made sense to him. He wasn't in a real happy place like last week. This was a struggle that seemed to zap all of his remaining strength. His feet are so swollen that they look like two big bags of cement attached to the ends of his skinny legs. 'My love' is my pet name for him, I use it often. Today I think "Goodbye, my love."

Dear Diary:

That was last week. Today he is waiting, bright and alert watching television and talking about Tiger Woods. He makes not one mistake as far as confusion goes, as a matter of fact amazes us with his memory. We cried all the way home last week and laughed all the way home this week. He's waiting for something, but he did tell me he was ready to go. I have this gut feeling he's waiting for Bob. I talked to Karen and she said they were going to Bonnie's for Christmas and would pop in to see him sometime during the day, then if he seemed stable would start packing for Florida. Dad wants his children all in one place, which is no easy task. He needs to know where we are.

He asked me to buy him some socks and pick off the dead leaves on the plant. He asked Ralph to straighten a picture, fix the time on the clock and just generally clean the room up. He was happy and joking and stayed awake the entire time, in spite of the drugs.

CHAPTER VI

BACK TO THE EARTH

December 28, 2009

The phone rang at twelve-twenty in the morning. A ringing phone in the middle of the night is the greatest fear of a mother, grandmother, and in this case, a daughter. The first thought I had was that he'd fallen again. By the time I fumbled around in the dark and answered it was too late. I called the nursing home and the night nurse told me, with both sadness and a trace of surprise in her voice, that my father had passed away in his sleep.

I lay in my bed and waited, waited for the hurt to creep in, the sadness. My brain made a quick calculation of the date. My father died on the twenty-eighth. If they called at twelve-twenty did he really die after midnight or before which would make it the twenty-seventh of December? It was a question that I never bothered to ask. I woke Ralph and we got up and drank coffee and talked. We didn't' cry. I felt peaceful, calm. It was the kind of peace that comes when you see and feel beauty until it almost becomes a physical ache, and you know that all is well in your world.

When my Mom died I was so shocked that I literally looked for her, searched for her in my dreams, during my daily walks, staring at the stars at night. With Dad's death it was all so easy, because I knew that it was his time, and he chose to go.

When the nursing home called Ron to say that Dad had died, he and Dixie had to go in to sign papers. The nurse told them that she would put a couple of chairs in the room so that they could have a few minutes alone with Dad. This was the last thing that Ron wanted. The thought of being in a room with his dead father was not a memory that he wanted to keep, but when he looked at his face, Dad looked exactly the way they had seen him sleep a hundred times before. So Ron and Dixie sat with him and talked about his life and his impact on their lives. Ron told me later "It got to a point where we forgot that he was lying in the bed right next to us. We just talked and talked. It was one of the best experiences of my life."

Dad had asked Karen on Christmas day when they were going away, and she said around the twenty-ninth so he died on the twenty-eighth. He planned it all out, he knew when to go, and that's why he had asked Ralph to straighten his room three days before. He waited until he knew that we three were ready for him to leave and didn't disrupt anyone's Christmas. These are the things he would think about before leaving.

The funeral was not the wonderful send-off that we had imagined, and it's not like we didn't have time to plan it. It was a bit of a disaster. The first real blizzard of the year hit, and it was a doozy. I was surprised at how few were there for a man who had been involved in every aspect of the community for his entire adult life, but, when you reach ninety-five most of your dearest friends have passed on and the others are not able to drive in a blizzard.

Before the service I noticed a woman standing in front of the casket. She was crying. When I introduced myself she said, "Your father changed my life." She went on to explain that her mother has Alzheimer's disease and was so terrified of the nursing home she wouldn't leave her room. She was afraid to go down for meals. The woman was telling Dad about the situation one afternoon and he said not to worry, he'd look after her mother and see that she got back and forth at mealtime. So three times a day he would wheel to her room and she'd put her frail hand on his wheel chair and he'd take her down to the dining room and wait for her, then take her back to her room. One of the nurses told the daughter that they were often the last two in the dining room. Dad always waited and the days he couldn't go down he would ask the nurses to make sure she was looked after. The woman told me that she could have a few moments of freedom from worry, knowing that Dad was looking after her Mom, and that three times a day her Mother didn't feel frightened.

And then, frail, being held up by his daughter and a nurse from the home, entered Walt. I was so touched and thanked him so much for coming. He replied, "I wanted to do it for Stew." His coming couldn't have been easy for his daughter or the nurse. Walt had a lot of difficulty walking and needed a great deal of assistance.

Just before they closed the casket, before the beginning of the service, I went to my Father to say good-bye. I held his cold hands and stroked his silky hair for the last time. People often say that a casket contains only an empty shell, say that their loved ones have already gone, but this was no empty shell. Sure his inner being, that magnificent mind had left, but this was a body that had served him well for over ninety-five years. I was thinking about all of this when I felt a presence beside me. It was my sweet Brandon, our only grandson, shy and unsure at the difficult age of fourteen. I thought, "Here is another one, one that will be a better person, more charitable, more tolerant and more loving because of the man lying in this simple casket."

Bob and Karen, Ralph and I and Ron and Dixie sat in unity at the front of the chapel, the way I had always pictured it in my mind. At times during Dad's dying process we had disagreed about his care and had almost become fractured as a family, but we were too strong, too united and all of one mind when it came to our love for our father. We were deeply affected when the soloist sang Dad's favorite hymn 'How Great Thou Art'. How can a song, an old hymn from our childhood, be almost painful in its simple beauty?

The eulogies were heart felt and poured love and respect. Mathew talked about memories of his grandfather. How Mat managed to visualize those days so long ago, and take the congregation back with him amazed me and left me greatly impressed. Brian, Dad's nephew and Aunt Mary's son, spoke about dad's many accidents. As somber as a funeral is supposed to be, at one point you had to smile, and some people even laughed out loud at the frequency of potentially life threatening episodes. Brian ended by saying how remarkable it was that this man had lived to the age of ninety-five.

It was still storming outside and there was a great deal of confusion as everyone got their coats. His six grandsons were pall bearers, as he'd requested. It was horrible at the grave site, blowing and snowing but most of all freezing cold. I shivered in my leather coat cursing myself for going the way of style instead of warmth. My family gathered around me like a protective, human garrison. Kelly's strong hand on my shoulder, the granddaughter's each holding a piece of me, just to let me know they were there. The men, my wonderful men, Phil and Brandon watching, making sure I was o.k. and Ralph, my love, holding me steady and trying to protect me from the wind. They would've been surprised and even mystified to know that I felt strong, almost invincible.

Unlike Mom, my Dad hadn't gone anywhere. I didn't have to spend time searching for him. He stayed. Trying to explain it is impossible and I don't feel the need to even try. All I can say is that he is always in my mind whether he's giving me hell for bad decisions or giving me answers when I find myself confused and lost in this difficult life. On a stormy day, I see him, hunched over, concentrating hard, straightening nails. Other times when I get tired of the struggle and I feel alone, though surrounded by people, my heart aches for the feel of his arms around me and I want so badly to just return to a time when it was all so simple and the only comfort I needed were my toes in his pocket.

EPILOGUE

When I'm feeling lonely or drifting away from the lessons my Father taught me, we take a drive down to Aurora, to the place where Mom and Dad used to live. A home where we shared so many memories around the dining room table, the place my Mother died. A fire hall now sits where the house used to be and just east of it a huge arena boasting two pools and three ice surfaces, a day care, gym and all the facilities of a modern complex.

Today my pace quickens as I head toward the park,' The Stewart Burnett Park', and I steer north toward the wetlands, past baseball diamonds and bleachers, towards the old pond. I follow paths the way I first did as a child and then as a grown up, but these aren't cow paths, they are man paths. The pond's frozen over right now. I wonder how high it will be in the spring surrounded by gardens and new trees. The air will be filled with the sound of children, playing on the slides and swings, parents cheering their little ones at baseball. I know as I return to the car that it is as it should be.

My father chose to sell to the Town of Aurora even though many other offers came his way. As he said, he had always been part of the community and "They always treated me well." Give back.

That's the Scottish way, the Stewart way.

THE ACHIEVEMENTS OF STEWART BURNETT

Member of the Whitchurch and Aurora area farming community for over 60 years, first at Preston Lake, then Victoria Square and Aurora Road—where they settled in 1952

Elected to the Vandorf School Board in 1949—spent 6 years in service with the Board

Elected to Hartman School Board in 1955—spent 9 years in service with the Board, including multiple terms as Treasurer

Ran for Whitchurch Municipal Council in 1961—served as councillor for 8 years, never losing an election

Elected "Top Councillor" in 1962

Spent 2 years as Deputy Reeve of Whitchurch Township

Spent 3 years as the Reeve of Whitchurch Township, including the honour of being the last Reeve in the Whitchurch Township history

In 1970 was elected by York County Council as the 1st Commissioner to the Warden

In 1972 was appointed to the Committee of Adjustments, Town of Aurora

Served for 8 years as a member of the Aurora Cemetery Board of Governors

Member of the Viking Sterling Club for 25 years

Initiated in 1959, was a member of the Masonic Rising Sun Lodge for over half a century; honoured as a Life Member.

Member of the Wesley United Church for over 60 years; where my mother's family were founding members

At Wesley United served on the Board of Governors, was Chairman of the Manse committee and was the Central Treasurer for 23 years; later he served as one of its Trustees; and I should not forget, dutiful church handyman

Won the Silver Tray for "Best Kept Farm" from York County, for his farm on Aurora Side road

On his Aurora farm, raised, bought and sold Holstein cattle as far as Florida, Vermont, California, Mexico and Cuba

Raised and showed Belgium heavy horses, perennial prize winners at the Schomberg, Aurora and Markham horse shows.

With one prize mare, in 1979, a first place ribbon and "Best in Show" honours at the Royal Agricultural Winter Fair.

Drove cancer patients to Sunnybrook hospital for over 20 years

Saturday, October 28 there was a ceremony at the new arena to unveil the sign for the future 'Stewart Burnett Park.

ACKNOWLEDGEMENTS

I need to thank my brothers and 'sisters' who were always there to answer my questions when my memory clouded over; and for not once asking what was going to be written about them, for trusting me.

To my children Kelly and Philip I thank you for your technical support and patience.

My very deepest gratitude goes to my husband Ralph who drove such a long distance, every week for eight years, so that I could see my father. This in itself goes beyond the marital call to duty.

When the storms hit, your strong hand kept me from being washed out to sea.

You were then and are now, my anchor.